play
ful

play
ful

How Play Shifts Our Thinking, Inspires Connection, and Sparks Creativity

· · · · · · · · ·

Cas Holman

With Lydia Denworth

AVERY

an imprint of Penguin Random House

New York

AVERY

an imprint of Penguin Random House LLC
1745 Broadway, New York, NY 10019
penguinrandomhouse.com

Copyright © 2025 by Cas Holman
Penguin Random House values and supports copyright. Copyright fuels creativity,
encourages diverse voices, promotes free speech, and creates a vibrant culture. Thank you
for buying an authorized edition of this book and for complying with copyright laws by not
reproducing, scanning, or distributing any part of it in any form without permission. You
are supporting writers and allowing Penguin Random House to continue to publish books
for every reader. Please note that no part of this book may be used or reproduced in any
manner for the purpose of training artificial intelligence technologies or systems.

Avery with colophon is a trademark of Penguin Random House LLC

Most Avery books are available at a discount when purchased in quantity for sales
promotions or corporate use. Special editions, which include personalized covers, excerpts,
and corporate imprints, can be created when purchased in large quantities. For more
information, please email specialmarkets@penguinrandomhouse.com. Your local
bookstore can also assist with discounted bulk purchases using the Penguin Random
House corporate Business-to-Business program. For assistance in locating a
participating retailer, email B2B@penguinrandomhouse.com.

Book design by Daniel Brount

Illustrations and hand-lettering copyright © by Cas Holman

Library of Congress Cataloging-in-Publication Data has been applied for.

ISBN 9780593713402
eBook ISBN 9780593713464

Printed in the United States of America
1st Printing

The authorized representative in the EU for product safety and compliance
is Penguin Random House Ireland, Morrison Chambers, 32 Nassau Street,
Dublin D02 YH68, Ireland, https://eu-contact.penguin.ie.

To the misfits, the outcasts, and the weirdos.
Stay brave.

CONTENTS

part one
why play?

THE CONDITIONS FOR PLAY

When I was growing up in Northern California, my front yard was full of ponderosa pines. Most days after school, I would hang out in one of those glorious trees. I loved it up there. My perch provided a different perspective. I left the human world, with its homework and chores, and joined the birds and bugs in their busywork. The ants would parade up and down in the brittle crevices of the bark, and I'd watch them frantically stepping out of the line to get around my hand or inspect some sap. That bark fascinated me as much as the ants. I understood the bark was the tree's skin, and while I climbed, I made a game of trying not to break it off or cause too much chaos for the ants. I didn't want to hurt the tree. I would sit up there for hours, or for what felt like hours to a six-year-old. Eventually, my mom would realize she hadn't seen me in a while and yell out the front door the way parents in rural America did in the '70s. "Set the table for dinner!" Sitting in that tree watching the world unfold below is one of my fondest play memories.

Even now, decades later, play is part of my life. In part, that is because I am a playful adult. But it is also because play is my work. I design for play. In 2011, for instance, I designed a play feature for the High Line Park in New York City. Then called the High Line Children's Workyard Construction Kit, now known as Rigamajig, it's essentially a set of loose construction materials: wood planks and pieces, large plastic bolts. The bolts are made for little hands to manipulate. Some of the planks are big enough that kids must work together to use them ("You hold this while I attach that"). No tools required and no instructions provided. Like all my work, Rigamajig was designed to be open-ended, to inspire play that allows children to figure it out, and to follow their own interests, ideas, and instincts. This is play that engages both the imagination and a desire to explore the world, using objects or one's own body. In other words, I design for what folks who work with kids call "free play."

Rigamajig has made its way into parks, schools, children's museums, and homes around the world. I've designed other playthings and play spaces that have been equally successful—like the Big Blue Blocks and Wobbly World, a play space for toddlers at Liberty Science Center in New Jersey. In 2019, I was featured in the Netflix documentary series *Abstract: The Art of Design*. I am immersed in play and, therefore, immersed in the world of children.

And yet, one of the questions I'm asked most often is: What about adults?

This question used to throw me. I didn't know where to begin and, to be honest, I couldn't imagine how to go about understanding (or even relating to) adults. The shelves in my studio are filled with books about playground design, woodworking, pedagogy, child development, and play in childhood. But the question was like a persistent hum in the background. It wouldn't go away. What *about* adults? When I finally began to give it some thought, I realized that as an art and design professor and as a consultant to various companies, I had been helping adults play for more than a decade. In fact, I had learned quite a bit about the dreams, needs, and motivations of people over eighteen. Once I was paying attention, I saw clearly how desperately adults need play in their lives. It's not a design problem. It's an adulthood problem. I could gather the most creative design minds and we could make a playground for adults, but I honestly don't think it would work. It's not about the space or the materials; it's about the adult. We don't need the right toy. We need the right perspective. We don't have to learn how to play; we have to *unlearn* how to *not* play.

I think I get asked about adults because, secretly, adults are jealous. When I use Rigamajig in the workshops I give for corporations like Google and Nike, participants tell me they wish they'd had Rigamajig when they were kids. (As a professor at Rhode Island School of Design [RISD], I wished my students had played with Rigamajig, too.) I tell people it's not too late. But that's a little bit of a lie. Adults—even art students—can't dive into a state of play the way a child can. We need to do some work first.

We're all born playful. We know how to play, but as we grow up, we learn to suppress those instincts. They get buried under rules and fears and assumptions about who we're supposed to be and how we're supposed to act as we approach adulthood. We become obsessed with productivity. Culturally, we allow the frivolity of play in childhood, but we are taught that it's something to grow out of as we age, that it's an activity we no longer need as we get a better sense of ourselves and our obligations multiply.

In adulthood, play is sanctioned in certain forms. We play pickleball and pickup basketball, World of Warcraft and Wordle. We listen to music and go to live shows. We flail around on dance floors and occasionally in our living rooms. We travel to Paris and Disneyland. We have sex. We even buy toys. My friends at LEGO and the German toy company Schleich (famous for true-to-life animal figurines) are hard at work designing products aimed at adults—recently coined "kidult" toys. I don't like that name because it implies that adults have to be kids in order to play, but it speaks to something larger, the fact that adults still want to play. Yet many of those adult toys are more like collector's items than toys. We assemble and display them or we never take them out of the package.

What I'm most struck by is that adults rarely engage in free play. When I design for free play, I have objectives—to inspire curiosity, creativity, innovation, and to encourage interaction, collaboration, and connection. I think about what materials can be used to invent a new game, or what materials can fit a range of moods. But in free play itself, there's no planned activity and no predefined outcome. For children, this comes naturally. But what about for us?

Free play happens when we do three things: embrace possibility, release judgment, and reframe success. It's a mindset shift, and under those conditions, whether we are kicking a soccer ball, singing pop songs, or sorting art supplies, we are driven by something internal rather than by external reward.

I believe that in the right context, state of mind, or company, we can all access that kind of play. A few among us already do. Painters play with color and line; poets, with words. All artists tap into imagination in their work and bring playfulness to the process. Comedians—both the professionals and the people we know who always make us laugh—are able to see the humor in the humdrum. They play without expectation. In a study of architects, psychologist Donald MacKinnon found that those considered most creative by their peers were those who knew how to play. He meant that they let themselves get absorbed in a problem for the fun of it, following their curiosity wherever it led. And at Cal Tech's Jet Propulsion Laboratory, when managers grew frustrated with a younger generation of workers who seemed to lack the problem-solving skills of their predecessors, the managers solved the problem by adding questions about childhood play to the interview process: Had they taken apart radios or clocks? Had they built things with their hands? If the answer was yes, the interviewees usually worked out once hired.

Letting ourselves get absorbed in play—free play—has benefits far beyond outcomes like making art, designing a beautiful building, or solving a problem in a laboratory (although those are worthy goals). The science of play has evolved along with my career, and it makes plain that being playful is critical for the well-being of both adults and children. I draw on those findings in my work every day. Play is how we learn to be human, how we learn who we are, how we learn to fail, communicate, love, fight, rebel, desire, build, survive. At its best, play is life-affirming, soul-sustaining, and mind-expanding. A life devoid of play is detrimental to our psychological, emotional, and physical health.

That is why I often tell the story about playing in a tree in my childhood front yard. I use play memories when I work with adults of all ages: Can you recall a moment of play from your own childhood? What was around you? What were the conditions? What did you feel? What made it possible? In the college classes I teach, young art students will turn to their sketchbooks, conjuring their memories as drawings. Their marks on the page help to bring out rich details in the setting. In the workshops I conduct for companies and organizations, members of the group turn to their neighbors and share what they remember, each weaving stories and finding similarities and surprise in the simplicity of the joyful scenes.

There is something striking about the memories that come up. They rarely involve a toy. They rarely involve adults. And they rarely involve an organized activity. A participant in one of my workshops described lining up rocks in a sidewalk gutter on a rainy day. She had started with marbles but kept losing them, so she switched to collecting rocks and arranging them into dams and sluices to see how that affected the trickle of water running by. Another in that workshop remembered hours spent with friends balancing on a broken door that had fallen over, creating a sort of seesaw they could all (almost) fit on. Another person loved hiding in a secret closet under the stairs with a best friend. And a remarkable number of us remember playing in the back seat of the car on long drives. Each memory is an example of free play, a moment when we did what we wanted, got caught up in it, and didn't want to stop. We remember the free play because it resonated deeply and stuck with us.

THE COMPLEXITY OF PLAY

"Trying to define play is like trying to define love," says play theorist Gordon Sturrock. "You can't do it. It's too big for that." But let's try anyway. Let's play with the definition because it's a helpful exercise. Sturrock is right: Play is big, but there are smaller, recognizable parts to it. Or to put it another way, different play types represent different play values—that's the term that play experts use to describe children's play. These categories are useful when designing for play, and in beginning to understand the complexity of it. The following are a few examples—not a complete list—based on the ideas of play expert Bob Hughes as handed down to me by Penny Wilson, one of the leaders of a group of professionals called playworkers. Playworkers oversee adventure playgrounds, also known as junk playgrounds in the UK and have made play their work but also their cause. They are highly trained, skillful facilitators of child-directed free play.

PLAY TYPES

- **Rough and Tumble Play:** Engaging physically with another person's body, testing strength, tickling, wrestling, play fighting.

- **Creative Play:** Making things (digital or analog), exploring materials, transforming this into that, often without defined outcomes.

- **Imaginative Play:** Pretending to be something or somewhere, inventing worlds and stories not bound by reality.

- **Dramatic Play:** Performances, impromptu acting out of scenarios, reenacting stories that the participants weren't involved in.

- **Locomotor Play:** Embodied play, experimenting with movement and the body.

- **Object Play:** Engaging and experimenting with the properties of an object.

- **Role Play:** Exploring ways of behaving, acting as someone or something other than oneself or one's lived experience.

- **Social Play:** Engaging and interacting with peers and exploring social hierarchies and dynamics.

- **Communication Play:** Using words, nuance, or gestures to explore language and understanding; to joke, sing, debate, rhyme.

- **Deep Play:** Encountering risky or even dangerous experiences, to develop survival skills and conquer fear.

- **Exploratory Play:** Curiously engaging objects and scenarios to understand them.

- **Mastery Play:** Controlling and repeating an activity or movement in an effort to level up.

Each of these categories of play can manifest in structured play or free play. To understand the difference, I turn to Penny's words. She describes free play as a set of behaviors that are "freely chosen, personally directed, and intrinsically motivated."

Let's unpack those critical elements.

Free play is freely chosen, i.e., it's voluntary. No one drags us into it or assigns it. Whatever it is we are doing is something we want to do, are even eager to do. It could mean lying on the couch with a book all afternoon or riding a bike for the feel of the wind in your hair or decorating cookies with some whimsy.

Personally directed play puts you in charge; it makes you the captain of your own play ship. The player or players make up the rules and goals (if any) as they go. You decide which book to read, where to go on your bike, or that you're going to make the Christmas cookies purple this year, just because.

And finally, anything that is intrinsic stems from our essential nature and is wholly part of us. *Intrinsic motivation* is our innate desire to do something for the sake of doing it, not for where it will take us. It is about the journey rather than the destination. *Extrinsic motivation* on the other hand is all about reaching goals and achieving rewards, getting external validation. In school, when you work for grades, everything becomes extrinsically motivated. Recent trends to "gamify" things like exercise and nutrition are adding extrinsic motivators. Too much focus on extrinsic motivation can mean you lose touch with whatever inner drive you had, and your focus shifts to an achievable, measurable goal.

Free play is what motivates my work. As a shorthand, I often describe myself as a toy designer, but I prefer to say I design for play. By that I mean that I design objects and spaces that create the conditions for free play to arise. I provide children with materials they can use to follow their instincts and get what they need from play. I give them tools, so they are free to imagine, explore ideas, and invent new things. The actor John Cleese said something similar about creativity: "You can teach creativity. Or . . . you can teach people how to create circumstances in which they will become creative." I want to create circumstances in which people will be inspired to be spontaneous, to be creative, to dare to make mistakes, and where they won't worry about rules because to the extent there are any, they made them up for themselves.

When I introduce myself as a toy designer, I learn a lot from people's responses. Everyone has associations and memories to share. A few years ago, I was at a conference in Palm Springs when I had an interesting exchange with a taxi driver who drove me back to the airport.

"How was your week?" he asked on the way. "What were you here for?"

I explained that I'd been giving a talk about my work, and I kept it simple. "I design toys," I said.

He was immediately skeptical. "When I was a kid," he said, "we didn't need all the fancy toys and hoopla. We just played."

He had my undivided attention "Oh yeah? Tell me about that," I said because I am always game to talk to strangers. (It's one way I play.)

"Well," he said, "there was a field. It wasn't a baseball field, but it became a baseball field. Whoever showed up at the field would play. Hopefully, the kid with the bat would come, but if he couldn't come, then we played without a bat. Sometimes there were seven kids. Sometimes there were three kids. Sometimes there was a twelve-year-old and a six-year-old, and sometimes we were all about the same age. No matter how many kids there were, we would make up a game based on who showed up and what we had. We weren't all necessarily friends. And nobody organized it. Whoever was around and didn't have chores came together and invented a game to play."

That was free play.

1 EMPTY LOT WITH BIG TREE
(BRANCHES TOO HIGH TO CLIMB)

1 LONG STICK WITH BEND

ROCKS OF VARIOUS SIZES

5 KIDS TOTAL

1 TIRE

1 BASKETBALL (FLAT)

2 MITTS (R HANDED)

2 HOURS 'TIL SUNDOWN

WHY NOT ADULTS?

I design for children because it's intuitive to me. From an efficacy perspective, it's also where I can intervene. I call it an intervention because we are designing so much structure into kids' lives and filling up their days with so many "productive" activities, that it feels like an intervention to push back against that impulse to plan for them. During childhood is when I can have the biggest impact. In protecting childhood play, I'm safeguarding a child's primary tool for shaping who they'll be as an adult and advocating for a healthy process along the way.

Childhood is a special time in our lives, no question. Children have no pretense. They can see how silly the rules of adulthood are. Perhaps I relate to kids because I also see how silly our adult rules are—maybe because I'm queer and sensed from an early age that the rules of adulthood wouldn't quite work for me, the concept of normal never applied. I often hang out with kids, and I enjoy their company. But I don't romanticize childhood as a phase or state of being. I like children as complete individuals and get along with some more than others. I've even met a few I don't like at all, although fewer children fall into that category than adults. My point is, we've established unnecessary boundaries between childhood and adulthood that significantly impact our respect for play.

By refusing to uphold those boundaries, I don't just design for kids. I design—albeit indirectly—for adults. In protecting childhood, I'm also protecting children's future selves. I'm thinking about how they will approach the world as adults. Many if not most early education programs are constructivist, meaning that in early childhood education, we let children learn by doing. Why do we think learning that way stops at the age of six? Humans are constructivist learners throughout life. We learn from doing at every age. We learn from play at every age. To put it another way, I design for play in childhood so that children can grow up and continue playing as they become adults. I aim to protect that state of playful thinking for everyone.

Yet, as a society, we seem intent on making sure adulthood doesn't include play. Think about sayings like "grow up" or "act your age" or "don't be childish." If a forty-five-year-old is throwing a tantrum that would rival a five-year-old's worst behavior, then sure, some of those sayings apply. Maturity does imply that you've developed better ways of channeling your anger than lying on the ground, kicking, and screaming. Having healthy play in childhood means that by the time we reach adulthood, we have fully developed theory of mind, which in turn means that we understand that the world doesn't revolve around us the way we thought it did when we were three.

But too often, if someone tells you to "grow up," what they are implying is that you're being frivolous, silly, or . . . playful. You are wasting time daydreaming. You're making jokes when you should be serious or productive.

Why is being silly a bad thing? Could silly be a tool to cope? Or daydreaming be a break for an overscheduled brain? We have come to believe that controlling our playful instincts is what makes us successful at adulthood. Feeling so happy you want to jump? So excited you want to scream? Finding the day so beautiful you want to romp outside? You can't. You're an adult. You learn to squelch those thoughts and get back to work, or go pick up the kids, or make sure you get groceries for dinner. We get so focused on the goal—whatever our priority is in the moment—that we run past the roses, the very thing that makes getting there enjoyable. Sometimes literally. I was once on a panel with a play researcher who described a moment when she was taking her four-year-old to day care on the way to work. They were late and the child stopped to look at some flowers. "Mommy, look how pretty!" And my colleague said, "We don't have time to smell the flowers." The irony was not lost on her. She immediately stopped in her tracks. She had become a play researcher who wasn't letting herself play.

It doesn't have to be that way. Too often, when we imagine playing as an adult, we think it should look the way it did when we were children. We expect to feel excited about playing the

same way we did in those play memories, with the same surroundings or toys. When we try to play this way, however, we
often find it isn't all that fun. I've had adults confess to me, usually in a whisper, that they don't have fun playing with their
children. They love being with them, but the play is a bit tedious
or boring. This makes so much sense! Of course it's boring, it's
not your play. You're playing with toys for children, and they're
not developmentally appropriate for you. That's not a concept I
love—*developmentally appropriate*—because it makes so many
assumptions about what is normal. But in this case, it's apt.
What's fun or challenging for a three-year-old or six-year-old, who
is just beginning to understand cause and effect or who is making
connections between ideas for the first time, is not necessarily fun
or appropriate for a thirty-three-year-old or a forty-six-year-old
who has lived in the world for some time. Adults have very different needs than children. Why would we play in the same way?

We adults can engage in a rich variety of forms of play. Like
children, sometimes we need to play quietly and lie in the shade
with some pebbles or a book. Other times we need to go run,
leap, jump, and slide. Most of those play types I mentioned
earlier—locomotor play, creative play, and so on—apply to adults
as well as children. What is a night out dancing if not locomotor
play, "movement in any and every direction for its own sake"?
And adults engage in role play every time they attend a Comic
Con convention and potentially in the bedroom, too.

But it strikes me that adults engage in some of our own types
of play that are a little different from what children do. Play for
children is developmental. It is part of what they need in order
to grow their brains and their sense of self. They are learning to

socialize, strengthening cognitive skills, and becoming more physically adept. Adults are in a different phase of life. I hesitate to say any of us are fully developed, because adult brains are capable of change and growth throughout life. But by our mid-twenties, most of our brain architecture is laid down and, for sure, we are differently developed than young children. In adults, play is less about development and more about sustenance. It's like the difference between drinking milk as a child to help grow your bones and taking in calcium as an adult to maintain bone health. We adults need help sustaining our well-being.

Maybe that sustenance comes from meditative or slow play, which might mean finding or creating order in a set of tools or doing yoga. Or maybe you find it in problem-solving play, as in visiting escape rooms, tinkering with cars, and completing puzzles, activities that occupy our minds enough to both calm and challenge. Our forms of identity play and role play allow us to escape our routine lives and become someone else. What else is drag, Renaissance fairs, and Halloween? Through everything from bungee jumping to horror films, we also use play to flirt with danger and explore taboo fantasies. Then there is playing around the edges of what's socially acceptable—what I call (mis)behavior play. Occasionally, when I'm overworked or generally stressed, a night out with friends will become more rambunctious than planned. This is to say, we "go hard." Once the night is in motion, I'll justify it as a necessary release valve—from working too much, feeling stressed in the city, etc. Still, it would be great if I could release pressure in a way that isn't as bad for my body or that doesn't have such negative repercussions the next day. It's curious that so many of us need to be drunk (or otherwise intoxicated) to really cut loose. Burning Man comes to mind—a utopian play party fueled by creativity, but also by mind-altering substances. We'd enhance our day-to-day if somehow we could bring those playful approaches to having collective experiences into our lives, without need for such extreme removal from reality.

I'll say more about these adult play types soon. What's important here is to understand that they exist and to see where free play fits into all this. Free play is an approach, it's a way of engaging with just about any type of play. On the other hand, much of what people call play doesn't qualify as free play. Inventing a game with a ball and two friends at a bus stop is free play; organized sports are not. Playing in the sand at the beach is free play; board games are not. A spontaneous dance party in the living room after dinner is free play; going to the theater is not. Don't get me wrong—I love theater and board games. They have plenty of benefits, many of us find them fun, and they can be good for our relationships, our bodies, and our minds. They satisfy some of the play types I just mentioned. But free play has value, too. In fact, I'd say it's essential. And because it's a little harder to spot, because by its very nature it is *not* organized or scheduled or measurable, it can be harder to access and benefit from in our lives.

Remember that definition of play as freely chosen, personally directed, and intrinsically motivated? Those elements are significant for children because what young people lack in their lives is agency. It means something different for them to choose an activity than it does for an adult to do so. We need the opposite. We have too much control and we need to let some of it go. We are fixated on goals, on outcomes. We need to let those go, too. We need to enter into play without an awareness of how we will look, how we will be perceived. Adult play requires a different permission structure (for us, and for each other) than we currently have. It means recognizing that play is not the opposite of productivity. To engage in free play, adults need to ignore some social rules, the ones that limit what it is to be grown-up. That takes extra work. Kids don't worry about acting weird in public, or dancing along to the TV, or imagining that their action figure is alive and climbing the subway pole. They have not yet learned to refrain from such activities. Adults have. That's what keeps us from going all the way into play. We have to give ourselves permission to play.

Adult free play happens when we do the three things I mentioned earlier: embrace possibility, release judgment, and reframe success. It is inherently vulnerable and non-hierarchical. It requires trust in oneself and one's surroundings. It is unattached to outcomes.

Free play means not just making room in our houses for "kidult" toys but making room in our lives for unstructured tinkering. What if we embraced the Sunday morning dillydally? What if we celebrated the meandering, the dithering, the puttering, the dawdling about? It's not that we need to play like children. It's that we need to stop acting like adults. We should ignore all the reasons *not* to play and leap in.

KICK OFF YOUR SHOES

These days, I regularly speak to and work with adult groups. I have talked to teams from companies including Google, Nike,

Ford, and Disney Imagineering. I've run workshops for foundations, museums, and universities around the world. I often bring Rigamajig. Those workshops are generally designed to influence how participants lead their teams or approach their process. The goal is to see one another anew and recharge their innovative spirit. And I'm happy to help with that. As a by-product, I hope they have a moment where they reconnect with play and remember that it's valuable. From there, in their lives as people who make decisions that often have broad impact, I hope they will value play in childhood.

But the workshops are about more than that. They serve as a pep talk for following your curiosity in adulthood. And as I've spent more time talking to adults about play, I've recognized a problem: Adults don't design their lives so that the conditions for play can arise.

In June of 2022, I was asked to lead a session at a conference put on by the Performance Theatre in London. They organize an annual gathering for leaders from all sectors of society—CEOs, foundation presidents, high-level government officials, artists. The event is a few days of workshops, panels, and conversations around London designed to spur innovative thinking, and this one had the theme of "our shared spaces." The underlying goal, really, was to generate high-impact thinking and work around climate change.

As with the other workshops I've led, the frame of my session in London was to get people to work without a defined outcome in mind. My theme was liminal space—meaning transitional places, or phases that lie in the in-between. Play is a great way to explore what can be discovered when we're in undefined territory. The organizers had been interested in the open-endedness of my work and how that approach might inspire other leaders. I saw it as an opportunity to bring people into the unexpected and help them be comfortable there. What seems to be the striking experience for participants—in that session and everywhere else I've done this—is that they play. Secretly, that's my goal. I distract them with some philosophical framework, a prompt, teamwork, and an abstract amount of time, and without noticing it, they are playing. I give them permission to depart from the performance of professionalism. I remove hierarchies. The materials are unfamiliar enough that they don't feel an intense need to be "good at them."

I serve as a kind of play coach.

In London, I broke them into groups of three, each with a pile of Rigamajig parts, and gave them this instruction: *Create a way to live in a cloud.* I use the word "create" deliberately instead of "build." It is more open-ended. The word "build" immediately calls to mind a structure, which is too limiting, whereas you can create anything.

You have eighteen minutes, I said. That's deliberate, too. It's not fifteen minutes, or twenty, but eighteen. It's a limited amount of time and one they aren't familiar with. I do that so they don't have time to plan. They have to jump in and figure out what they are making while they are making it. They have to play.

Name it and be prepared to think about how you'll tell the story, I added when they had three minutes left. Again, this is deliberate. I intentionally frame the retelling exercise as a story rather than a presentation. The word "presentation" is loaded with professional baggage and carries pressure and the need to perform

21

in front of colleagues. Telling a story is looser and more fun. Usually, the story emerges in the moment they are telling the group about it. I prompt the group with "Yes and . . ." questions, and invite them to ask, "What if . . . ?" An improvisational collaborative imagining unfolds.

It isn't always easy for people to get started. The group in London was no different. Many told me they rarely worked with their hands or made things. I sensed they were surrounded by peers they respected but didn't know very well. In such situations, there's an element of self-criticality that makes people feel vulnerable. We anticipate the criticism of others. That's often why we're so afraid of failure, why we're hesitant to wade into the unknown or embark on something new that we might be bad at. What would feel like straightforward play for a kindergartener makes these talented overachievers stiffen with fear.

But as the minutes ticked by, I wandered the room and I saw change happening. As people engaged and enjoyed the materials, they went from comparing credentials to creative problem-solving. They forgot to worry about being judged. They were having too much fun to judge others. They helped and got help from their team members. Five minutes in, I saw and heard flow. Creative flow, collaborative flow, imaginative flow . . . the flow of play.

Some of them got on the floor. Some of them took off their jackets and even their shoes. That is the moment I know I've succeeded.

Always, I give them a few minutes' warning when the time is almost up. If they're really engaged, I admit I let them go a little longer than I said I would.

When time was up, each group took a turn telling the story of their creation. "This is a cloud mole machine . . ." one group said, demonstrating all the parts of their machine and explaining how it worked. "This is a robot who can lift you into a cloud . . ." another group offered.

At the end, I was very transparent. "You are wonderful, and I tricked you into playing," I told the group. As is often the case, they seemed to feel great. Many of them wanted to hang out, to stay and keep playing and talking. Talking to me afterward, there are always a few who express surprise that they played at all or surprise at how it made them feel. But they're energized. "I was in it," said a man in a bespoke suit. When they did walk away, they walked away having remembered how to play, if only for an hour and a half. They had reconnected with their younger selves—the selves who prioritized play.

In the episode of Netflix's documentary series *Abstract* that features me and my work, I'm very open about my own struggles in school and to be seen and accepted for who I am. After it aired, my inbox was flooded with messages.

"After watching . . . I realized I had lost the joy of playing."

"The show opened the door for me to reconcile with my childhood."

I think my visible lack of regard for adult rules resonates with people. They get emotional telling me about it, and sometimes I get emotional listening. Ignoring those norms is so natural for me now that I don't think about it much. But I've been known to cry when I hear from people who are struggling, and I catch a glimpse of how oppressive it is to not be able to be yourself. Those messages in my inbox are a testament to this.

"I've been struggling with how I fit into this whole puzzle of a world."

"I've never felt understood, so I took refuge in the family I imagined with my dollhouse."

"As a teen I was so focused on 'being good' and competing that I lost the inspiration and the joy of the sport I loved."

Some messages are so full of pain and rejection, they are frankly heartbreaking.

Play taps into our authentic selves but those selves don't always align with the community we find ourselves in. Maybe you love to fix things but grew up in a household that honors intellect and doesn't know how to support or understand your passion for internal combustion engines. Perhaps you have eccentric tendencies and express yourself in ways that others deem "extra." When we acknowledge that play is a way into who you are, we reframe such experiences and retell our own stories, and sometimes we widen our possibilities, too.

When we're children, we're attuned to our instinct to play, and we get what we need from play. It serves us incredibly well then, and I believe it can continue to serve us in adulthood. I think the reason those play memories people share in my classes and workshops are so evocative is that they recall free play, and they also represent something that is missing from our adult lives. My goal in helping you reconnect with your play is that the next time you remember your play, it will be not from childhood, but from last week.

2

PLAY IS IN US

F ar down the western coast of Africa, close to Walvis Bay in Namibia, there is a spot among the sand dunes where archaeologists found something rare: astonishingly well-preserved footsteps in a patch of dry mud. Such ancient footprints are cause for excitement in archaeology because they connect us so viscerally to the people of the past—we get a glimpse of their behavior, of their movements. Those people could have been us. These tracks, which date from about 1,500 years ago, were made by a small group of children. There may have been as many as nine kids ranging in age from four or five up to thirteen or fourteen. The children were walking along behind a flock of sheep or goats—the animals' hoofprints are also preserved. That suggests the kids were working, tending to the family or community herd.

From the pattern of the footfalls, the archaeologists can see more than that. Although everyone in the group was moving together in a general way, there are abrupt changes of direction here and there and "a lack of linearity to some of the trails." In a few spots, only the ball and toe of a foot show up. In others, only the heel. The scientists' conclusion? The kids were hopping, skipping, and jumping as they worked. In other words, they were being "playful," wrote Professor Matthew Bennett of Bournemouth University in the United Kingdom, who, along with his colleagues, analyzed the prints. These were traces of play.

It's fun to think of this group of children playfully crisscrossing the muddy plain so long ago, refusing to walk in a straight line just for the fun of veering off course. I imagine them leaping and spinning, stopping, and starting, and the older ones herding the younger ones along with the sheep, hopefully doing some jumping and running themselves. I imagine them all laughing and calling out to one another in the dusty sunlight, arms flung wide, following nonlinear paths. Playing. The footprints have captured something intangible and timeless. They are a still life of joy.

It's no surprise those kids were playing. Of course they were. Play is ancient. It's evolutionary. Play is in us and always has been.

I was reminded of that in powerful ways during the Covid-19 pandemic. In January of 2020, I took on a new commission for the Liberty Science Center in Jersey City, New Jersey. The design brief was to overhaul a 3,000-square-foot space to create a place where children under five could explore balance.

Until then, I hadn't designed extensively for toddlers, so I dove into research about early childhood. I toured playgrounds to observe spaces that were engaging these little ones, and I have to say, toddlers are wonderful! They fall all day long. They are so good at falling, I'm not convinced their goal is to stay upright. They're more comfortable on their butts or their bellies than they are on two legs. Watching them, I stopped assuming a fall was a fail. When toddlers went from vertical to horizontal, they would often just hang out where they landed, saying, *Cool, now I'll play with this leaf.* Or, *Hey! There are rocks down here! I'm gonna inspect every single one. I wonder what they taste like. Will they fit in my nose?*

That toddler's-eye view of the world shifted my thinking on balance. Balance is not perfection or symmetry. Balance isn't level, it isn't stasis. It is a constantly shifting ebb and flow of forces acting against and with each other. It is all the interconnected strands in the web of life—people, ideas, movements—that tug us back and forth. And sometimes balance means learning how to fall and maybe even how to hang out where you land, observing new things and saying, "Cool!"

I was only a few months into the ideation phase of this new project when the pandemic hit. The world went into a state of extreme uncertainty, and we stayed there. Children grew up there. Comfort in uncertainty made its way into my design brief. Uncertainty is inevitable, so I decided to embrace its inherent playfulness. You can't control everything, but you can play with unpredictability. That's what the design of the space at Liberty Science Center does.

Called Wobbly World, it opened to the public—with pandemic restrictions in place—in December 2021. It is a place where process, exploration, and curiosity are valued over outcome and mastery of skill. The exhibit inspires children to play with abstract objects and seemingly incomplete, imperfect surfaces. By using their bodies to interact with unfamiliar forms, they experience balance as a fluctuating state, affected by the movement of everyone in the room. Everything in the space is intentionally off-kilter. In a far corner, odd-shaped foam blocks—full of curves, teeth, wedges—fit into custom holes in the wall (because cleaning up is part of the fun). Although I usually design so kids can make anything, I designed these blocks with the opposite goal—it is not possible to make any specific "thing" with them. What you can do is coax them into precarious stacks that echo the exuberant landscapes of Dr. Seuss books, or you can line them up to make uneven obstacle courses that call to mind a jumble of uneven rocks across a stream.

Uncertainty also informs the iconic piece in the space. Inspired by Alexander Calder's mobiles and stabiles, I designed a giant mobile where the children's bodies become the moving elements. Each of its ten hanging swings is activated by movements made on the adjacent swing as well as those across the room—you can't spin until the person opposite bounces, which makes two people sway over there. Everyone's playing separately and together—my movements, my play impacts yours.

I can describe it all easily now. But designing the project during the pandemic was anything but easy. Of course, the logistics of working with a team that couldn't be in the same room were challenging. More significantly, the pandemic influenced my conceptual thinking. At first, it felt bold to talk about comfort with uncertainty and to recognize that balance isn't about symmetry. As the pandemic dragged on, it felt obvious. Duh. Uncertainty was everywhere. Acknowledging that life is messy—that you yourself are sometimes a hot mess—felt edgy before and normal after.

But I also think it was a huge relief for most of us not to have to pretend everything was perfect at home anymore. The pandemic was a reset. Suddenly we could imagine holding a meeting in our pajamas. Pets and noisy children became routine parts of our work lives rather than hidden parts of our private lives. We didn't have to perform adulthood with the same rigidity as before. Balance? What balance? I consoled myself with the knowledge that even if the idea of embracing uncertainty no longer felt original, it felt true.

Eventually, we built a prototype for the space and launched playtesting. That is when we have kids play with the designs to see how they actually use what we have created. We learn whether the designs appeal, whether they work as intended or function in unexpected ways. I love playtesting. It is like anticipating a response to a carefully chosen gift. Beforehand I'm excited (*what will they do with it?*) and nervous (*what if they hate it?*). This moment of launching something new into the world is a critical piece of the design process. You put your ideas out there and see how they fly.

Playtesting is a playful way to approach life in general. It requires staying open to possibility, to experimentation, to overturning preconceived notions. It works best when you are open to the likelihood that some of your favorite creations or ideas or plans just don't work the way you thought they would. When playtesting something with friends, it's a chance to let everyone off the hook, and just see how it goes. If the new activity is a bust, no big deal! No one is responsible for making sure it's great. The play is in trying it together and talking throughout about what could make it better as you go.

But playtesting during the pandemic hurt my soul. We had to tell kids they couldn't interact. *Don't touch the other kid's toy! Don't play with kids in that other family! Don't cross the tape line!* We had a room the size of a basketball court, and we divided it into four sections. Time slots were reserved by caregivers who brought their kids and they played with the materials in their dedicated section. We'd fabricated prototypes of fifty giant foam block shapes and made piles in each section. At some point in the day, a seven-year-old noticed that the block he really wanted was being used by another child in the adjacent section. They made eye contact, and from their body language I knew they were about to do what the blocks were designed for—play together. I quickly made my way to the tape line and met the seven-year-old just before he crossed. He looked at me sideways, then turned, dragging two unwieldy blocks behind him, and walked around the end of the tape to get to the other section. "I didn't cross it," he said, pausing for a moment to see how I'd react before grinning beyond the edges of his mask. He'd beat me at this game with absurd rules. I couldn't have been more relieved. Try as we might, we couldn't kill off the children's instinct to engage with each other. Even if play looked different in the moment, its core elements would survive. They had to! In the true spirit of playtesting, the tape, which I hadn't thought we were even testing, didn't work the way we thought it would but revealed something important, nonetheless.

I realized that what the pandemic meant for play was hard to separate from what the pandemic meant for humanity. We need to play and we need to connect. We need play in order *to* connect. Play relates to wellness, to community, to work, to family.

THE SCIENCE OF PLAY

I am far from the first person to argue that we need to respect play and acknowledge our playful instincts. That message has been repeated through the decades even if it hasn't always found a receptive audience. The disinterest in play says more about the priorities of the listeners than it does about the central importance of play. For anyone paying attention, there is a well of evidence backing up the argument.

Play is critical to the development of children. They use play to communicate before they have much other language to express themselves and they build and strengthen cognitive and social skills such as regulating emotion and sharing. Psychoanalyst Erik Erikson, a champion of the importance of play for children, called it a kind of "emotional laboratory" for experimenting and learning. In play, children don't have to worry about making mistakes. Play gives children a chance to master the world they inhabit and at the same time create, develop, and maintain a sense of self. Play is so essential for children that it is listed in the United Nations 1989 Convention on the Rights of the Child, which recognizes the right to rest and play.

Paradoxically, some of the very people who helped establish the importance of play for children were dismissive of it for adults. Erikson, for instance, observed grown-up play and noticed it looked phony and forced. "The adult . . . often seems to be playing at playing," he once said. Exactly! Because we are out of touch with our play! I have to wonder if he was watching adults play with children, or perhaps in some other way that wasn't their own play.

But there have been others who thought broadly about play, and who recognized its importance for adults. One of the first was the Dutch historian Johan Huizinga. In 1938, when he published his seminal book on play, *Homo Ludens*, it was quite radical to argue that play was a central organizing force in human culture. But that's what Huizinga did. "For many years the conviction has grown upon me, that civilization arises and unfolds in and as play," he wrote. Huizinga saw play permeating language, myth, and ritual, all of which he considered root forces guiding human societies. He also developed one of the first important and lasting definitions of play. He pointed out that play is fun, it is voluntary, it's a freedom. "We might call it a free activity standing quite consciously outside 'ordinary' life as being 'not serious,' but at the same time absorbing the player intensely and utterly," he wrote. That idea of absorption translates neatly to the more modern idea of "flow," introduced by psychologist Mihaly Csikszentmihalyi many years later. Flow, Csikszentmihalyi said, is a state in which people are "so involved in an activity that nothing else seems to matter." In adulthood, when we're talking about flow, we're often talking about play—whether we realize it or not. I design for play and I design for flow. Flow is what happened in London at the

Performance Theatre workshop, when adults got down on the floor and lost all track of time, and their shoes.

Anthropologists who followed Huizinga embraced his ideas. They recognized play as universal: There is no culture in the world that doesn't play. They recognized it as therapeutic: For more than a hundred years, therapists have made use of play to heal and work through trauma. And the anthropologists recognized that play was likely rooted in the evolutionary neurobiology of humans. Every day I see the truth in those three ideas—that play is everywhere, that it helps us strengthen what is broken or weak, and that the need for it is hardwired in our brains. That last point, the biological story of play, is especially compelling because, in a sense, everything else about play springs from there.

Play, we know now, shapes the brain. In the 1960s, a pioneering neuroscientist named Marian Diamond showed that for the first time by conducting a series of studies with rats. One group of rats was raised in cages full of toys, challenging mazes, and other rats to hang around with. The second group was raised in individual metal cages with no toys, no mazes, and no playmates. Diamond and her colleagues found structural and chemical differences in the brains of the rats in the "enriched" environment—the one with toys and companions. Those rats were smarter, and their brains were larger and more complex than the brains of the rats in the isolated condition. Diamond also showed that it was not just toys or playmates but the combination of the two that was essential. Because it was the 1960s and she was fighting to be taken seriously as a woman in science, Diamond stressed "enrichment" and avoided the word "play" to describe her findings. But, let's be honest, what the rats in the enriched cage were doing was playing with each other and with the toys and mazes they could explore each day.

What was happening in the rats' brains to make them larger and more complex? From the moment babies—rat babies, human babies, and just about every other kind of baby—are born, their brains build on experience. Each experience—the sight of their parent's loving face, the smell of a grandparent's cologne, the sound of their siblings zooming Matchbox cars, their own exploration of their toes, then their toys, then their town—alters the configuration of their young brains, sending electrical signals from one neuron to the next, creating networks that grow in size and efficiency the more they are used. Repeated experiences solidify those networks. As neuroscientists say, neurons that fire together wire together. Pretty soon, a baby recognizes its parent instantly, feels the contented knowledge that Grandpa is nearby from the familiar smell of his aftershave, and knows that shaking a rattle creates a delightful sound. In time, brain circuits will be created for movement, for language, for reading, and everything else that is ahead in life. When experiences don't occur—the grandparent doesn't wear cologne, to take a minor example—that particular set of connections won't be made, because neurons that aren't seeing any action get pruned away to keep our brains working efficiently. In this sense, brains are an excellent example of the use-it-or-lose-it principle. For Marian Diamond's rats, the play in the enriched environment elicited the animals' natural curiosity, their instinct to explore and experiment with what they found. Engaging in such activities strengthened connections between different areas of their brains.

Jaak Panksepp, another neuroscientist, picked up where Diamond left off, beginning in the 1970s. He was less hesitant to use the word "play" but admitted that doing so made it hard for him to get funding and to get others to take his work seriously. For a long time, science was "not quite ready to embrace a behavior that, at least on the surface, seemed frivolous, disorganized, and especially hard to quantify," his colleagues Sergio Pellis and Stephen Siviy wrote in a tribute to Panksepp.

Panksepp didn't start out studying play; he first studied attachment and the pain and anxiety of separation in rats, but he noticed that when his rats were hanging out in their cages, they would bounce and pounce, nuzzle and nip, wrestle and pin each other. "When you put them together, bang! They play," he said. "They played with such eagerness that I was blown away." He began to think that the underpinnings of play and laughter in the brain might be just as interesting and informative to study as the negative emotions of pain and anxiety. "If you understand the joy of play, I think you have the foundation of the nature of joy in general," he told *Discover*.

Years of play studies followed. Panksepp used periods of isolation to make the rats hungry for play (as so many of us are!). The longer rats went without play, the more intensely they engaged in it when they got the chance—so much so that Panksepp came to think of play deprivation as akin to thirst or hunger, an alarm signal that prompts us to seek out a missing essential. Then, taking a cue from his own kids, Panksepp started tickling his rats to encourage them to play, earning him the nickname "the rat tickler" in the popular press. That's how he worked out that the rats didn't only play, they laughed, making ultrasonic vocalizations when they were enjoying themselves.

Given how eagerly young rats "pursue the fun side of life," Panksepp suspected that play was embedded in a deep and primitive part of the brain, just as attachment is. To prove it, he removed the rats' neocortices, the outer layer of the brain responsible, in humans, for higher order thinking. Even without most of their neocortex, the rats played in a fundamentally normal way. That meant that play was a primitive process and most likely vital to survival. Panksepp eventually identified it as one of seven primary emotions, which he always spelled in all caps to indicate their importance: SEEKING, RAGE, FEAR, LUST, CARE, PANIC/GRIEF, and . . . PLAY. Such work made the neuroscience of play mainstream. It showed that play helps construct and refine many of the higher regions of the social brain. "Play allows us to stop, look, listen, and feel the more subtle social pulse around us," Panksepp said.

ENCOURAGING CURIOSITY AND CREATIVITY

That drive to stop, look, listen, and feel could also be called curiosity, which in turn is an essential element of play. What else is turning over a log to see what's underneath or peeking into a friend's refrigerator or pushing all the buttons in a rental car? In recent years, neuroscientists have gotten more curious about curiosity. "You can think of curiosity as the process that guides the acquisition of knowledge," says psychologist Celeste Kidd of the University of California, Berkeley, who studies the trait in people of all ages. In a world teeming with information, humans and other animals must gather what they need to know about their worlds to survive. They do this for practical reasons, such as the need to work out how to find food or how to earn money. But often we are intrinsically motivated to gather information just for the sake of knowing; we gather information because we are curious.

Yet even when curiosity doesn't have obvious benefits in the short term, it might well over the long term—curiosity makes evolutionary sense. Some of the studies that show this most clearly involve computers and algorithms. Let me try to describe one such experiment in noncomputing terms. Imagine your computer screen is divided into four sections, or "rooms," and within those rooms are two boxes of food randomly placed in the otherwise empty space. Now imagine you are playing a game that requires you to keep yourself fed. Whenever you are hungry, you enter the rooms on the screen to eat. But every time you're in there, the boxes are in a different spot, and you have to locate them. The boxes also require specific sequences to get them to open, so you must work out the trick to opening each box. But you can't simply leave a box open for the next time. If you do, the food inside will spoil. To get any nourishment, then, you must find a closed box, open it, and eat the food immediately, then reclose the box. Eating is necessary for survival, so each time you eat, you benefit. The researchers—remember these were computer scientists—worked out an algorithm to show that eating was good. Duh. But even better than eating, the researchers showed, was spending time "playing" with the boxes, manipulating them, and figuring out how they work even if you didn't get to eat each time you did that. Over time, the more you play, the more you'll eventually eat. "Richer kinds of behavior less directly related to basic needs, such as play and manipulation of the boxes . . . can confer significantly greater evolutionary fitness," they concluded. That takeaway neatly paraphrases a familiar saying: Teach people to open a box and they eat for a day; teach them to play and they eat for a lifetime.

Curiosity, then, helps our brains learn about complicated things. It helps us pick and choose which information in the sea of information that surrounds us is worth our attention. We do that, from infancy to adulthood, by looking for information that fits into a cognitive sweet spot: It's a little bit surprising but not too surprising. Humans aren't the only ones who are curious. Monkeys and mice are, too. Neuroscientists have shown that their brains recognize information as a distinct commodity, different from a physical reward such as juice or water. They also assign information value for its own sake. In experiments where the animals must make choices like whether to turn left or right (mice) or which box to choose on a touchscreen (monkeys) to *possibly* get a reward, both species will give up larger rewards in favor of gathering information ahead of time about whether there will be any reward at all.

We humans are "hypercurious." We learn by building on our natural bent for curiosity. That starts in brain circuits that are geared toward detecting what's new and different. Our brains seek novelty. From birth, an infant's sensory processes maximize novelty and surprise to boost learning. A rattle is interesting to a very young infant who is working out that moving the rattle causes it to make enjoyable noise. Older infants get bored with rattles because they know all about them. What is interesting depends on what you know. Recognizing that something is unusual is a way of expanding knowledge but also a way of protecting oneself from potential harm. Coming across a berry you don't recognize in the woods should make you curious as to what it is but also cautious about eating it without knowing whether it's poisonous.

When we do find something new, the brain's reward system kicks into gear—more evidence that curiosity has long-term benefits. Generally, our bodies and brains are designed to encourage behavior that helps us, so behavior that is rewarding is something we are likely to repeat. Curiosity also helps to reduce uncertainty. *What happens if I do this? How about that?* Think of a young child pressing buttons and pulling levers on a cause-and-effect toy to see what pops out or whether the music plays. Adults are no different; we've just moved on to be curious about other things. What happens if I add blueberries to these muffins or what if we move the couch over there? Much of what we do in the name of curiosity is play.

Play is also at the heart of human creativity. As a designer and an inventor, I am deeply invested in the value of creativity— for everyone, not just for other designers and inventors. I believe everybody should experience a creative life, especially children. Twenty years ago, my thinking gained clarity from the work of an education psychologist named D. W. Winnicott, an early thinker on the link between creativity and play. He was interested in how imagination is formed, and he looked to early childhood for insight into what helps people play and what *keeps* them from playing. He saw simple games of peekaboo with Mom as an essential foundation of a child's development. Among other things, such games were invitations to play in a safe place with a safe playmate. Both are essential for adults to play as well. Winnicott argued that our capacity for being—the ability to feel genuinely alive inside—is nurtured by childhood play, and that that capacity was necessary for finding and maintaining our true selves. Essentially, he was saying that play was at the core of our emotional and psychological well-being. "Playing facilitates growth and therefore health," he wrote.

Evidence for these ideas comes from a variety of studies by other researchers. Some of them were studying play explicitly, but more often, they were studying creativity, positive mood, pressured or unpressured situations, or some combination of those things. The results tell us a lot about playful thinking. For instance, pressure to perform well, to look good when assessed, interferes with new learning. And pressure to *be* creative interferes with creativity. Psychologist Teresa Amabile spent years studying what contributes to creativity in people of all ages. She and her colleagues invited children and adults to get creative—by making collages or writing poems. Some people were told ahead of time that their work would be judged, or they were asked to focus on extrinsic reasons for being creative (e.g., money or fame). Others were told prizes would be randomly awarded in a raffle or were asked to focus on their intrinsic motivation for being creative. The most creative efforts (as judged by experts including fine art students) consistently came when participants felt free of judgment, when they weren't thinking about external rewards, and when they felt encouraged to enjoy themselves. In work environments, Amabile found that the culture created by managers had powerful influence over the ultimate creativity of the projects generated by workers. High creativity was fostered in offices where people felt intellectually challenged, had sufficient resources, and were given greater freedom and where innovative thinking was encouraged by supportive bosses. The upshot of the research is that the more we direct someone to think creatively, the harder it is for them to do just that. Rewards don't help. They can prove motivating for rote tasks, but not for creative tasks. "Creativity is a spark that comes when mental conditions are just right," writes Peter Gray in his book *Free to Learn*.

What are those conditions? What does spark creativity? Playfulness. There is a well-known, early study by the late psychologist Alice Isen that points to this. In 1987, she showed that inducing a playful mood improves creativity and insightful problem-solving. Like many other researchers before her, Isen used Duncker's candle problem in which participants are given a small candle, a book of matches, a box of tacks, and a bulletin board. The challenge is to attach the candle to the bulletin board so that it burns, upright. Even elite college students rarely figure it out. (But you, reader, surely can! If you are stumped, the solution is in the Notes.) Isen divided her students into three groups. In the first, she induced a positive mood by having them watch a five-minute humorous video before presenting them with the problem. A second group watched a serious video clip while the third watched no film at all. Seventy-five percent of the students who watched the humorous video solved the problem compared to 20 and 13 percent of the students in the other two groups respectively. That positive mood that Isen created was a playful mood. Humor is playful, and in watching funny videos, the participants felt playful themselves and brought that spirit to their problem-solving. Inspired by her own results, Isen kept toys on her desk for colleagues to play with during long meetings on the grounds that it would keep her coworkers in a playful and therefore innovative frame of mind. In the same vein, people from an office down the hall from my studio regularly come to borrow toys to play with in their meetings.

Those were young adults—college students—Isen was testing, yet another reminder that playfulness helps adults, not just kids. Winnicott knew that well. "Whatever I say about children playing, really applies to adults as well," he wrote, "only . . . [it's] more difficult to describe." We are always developing, growing, evolving, and, at any age, play is crucial to that development. In adults, Winnicott believed, play shows up in our choice of words, in the inflections of our voice, in our sense of humor. But, too often, he noted, adults don't let themselves be playful. Or maybe they don't know how. "In a tantalizing way, many individuals have experienced just enough creative living to recognize that for most of their time they are living uncreatively, as if caught in the creativity of someone else or of a machine," he wrote. His conclusion: "In playing, and perhaps only in playing, the child or adult is free to be creative."

THE RISKS OF NOT PLAYING

In humans, the essential importance of play and the consequences of a lack of it were clarified by psychiatrist Stuart Brown, who ushered in the modern era of taking play seriously with his 2008 bestselling book, *Play*. I first learned of Brown's work at a conference in 2010. He spoke briefly, giving just a ten-minute introduction, but I was captivated and went home and found an online talk he had given called "Play Is More Than Just Fun" (since picked up by TED). It blew my mind. Here was a scientist who was passionate about play and had a fascinating story to tell about how he came to care about it.

In August 1966, Brown was a "newly minted" assistant professor of psychiatry at Baylor College of Medicine in Houston when a tragedy struck not far away at the University of Texas at Austin. An engineering student named Charles Whitman climbed a tower on campus and began shooting at people walking down below. Whitman managed to kill fifteen and wound thirty-one before being killed himself. It was the kind of crime that has become horrifyingly common now but then was highly unusual. Brown joined a group of doctors and mental health experts tasked with trying to understand Whitman's motivation and, more significantly, to see if it was possible to identify others who might be potential killers before they struck.

The group was not surprised to find signs of the trouble to come in Whitman's youth. His father had been severely overcontrolling and had abused his mother, both of which contributed to the development of Whitman's behavioral problems. But the thorough investigation of his whole life revealed a more surprising trigger. "After extensive interviews with everyone who had entered Charlie's life, it became clear that *the lifelong lack of play* [emphasis original] had itself been an important factor in his psychopathy," Brown wrote in *Play*. As a child, Whitman was never allowed to play freely or outside of the house. Even in preschool, Whitman didn't engage normally with other children.

Brown believed he and his fellow researchers were onto something and he began to take play histories from convicted killers. Again and again, he found an absence of play in their childhoods and found that that absence was as important a predictor of their crimes as any other factor. "Play is a necessary nutrient for us to survive well and not be toxic to each other," Brown has said.

As part of his research into play, Brown also spent time thinking about the parallels between human play and that of other animals. He once went out into the field with biologists in Alaska to watch brown bears. One day, two young males caught his attention. The pair "went in and out of the rapids, splashed through clear sparkling pools, circled, pirouetted, then stood and leaned against each other, embracing in an upright dance," he wrote. "Periodically they paused, looked at the water, and then, as if under the influence of a master conductor, set at each other mouth-to-mouth, head-to-head, paw-to-paw, in an agile display of bear play."

Of course, you don't have to go to the Alaskan wilderness to appreciate animals playing. Countless videos on social media capture them in action. Have you seen the viral video of a crow snowboarding down a snowy rooftop—again and again—on the lid of a jar? Or the BBC footage of dolphins batting around a puffer fish like a ball? For that matter, have you ever played fetch with a dog? Renowned biologist E. O. Wilson was convinced that even ants engage in play fighting, though I confess I didn't notice that during my hours watching them high in my tree.

In fact, it's very difficult to *stop* animals from playing. Play is in them just as it is in us. The play we see in so many other animals confirms that it serves a larger purpose. Play sharpens wits, it teaches how to navigate a social group, it helps prepare for adulthood through pretend rehearsal. For young children, play is all of that and more. It is how humans learn about the world and themselves. Play is also just plain fun. (That crow!) Although the specifics of play vary a bit from one species of animal to another ("herbivores run about and prance more, predators chase and wrestle"), what binds them together, Panksepp said, is "the overall impression of joyous lightness of being."

WITH WHATEVER (CON CUALQUIER COSA)

I've seen that same lightness of being that Panksepp described in places that are otherwise full of heaviness. It is more convincing evidence of the indefatigable, persistent nature of play. In the city of Reynosa, on the Mexican side of the Rio Grande River just south of Hidalgo, Texas, there are thousands of asylum seekers waiting to have their cases heard and to be able to cross into the United States. Many are Spanish speakers from Central or South America, but there are growing numbers of Haitians and Ukrainians now, too. All of them arrive in Reynosa with nothing but what they could carry when they left home. Many of them—on average, 50 percent—are under eighteen years old.

Once in Reynosa, the asylum seekers live in a series of camps. Some are makeshift, thrown up in the center of town, though most of those get torn down. Two are a little more permanent. Called Senda de Vida and Senda de Vida 2 (Way of Life), they were founded by Pastor Hector Silva and the Senda de Vida Ministry and built with the support of a nonprofit called Solidarity Engineering. These camps are an attempt to provide asylum seekers a safe place to live while they wait to hear their fate. Safety is a serious issue because the violence that drove many of the asylum seekers from their homes is present here, too. That's why the camp walls are 10 feet high, made of concrete block, and topped with barbed wire. Beyond safety, the two Senda de Vida camps aim to provide some sense of community and a little stability. Most of the adults take on unpaid jobs that support life in the camp—everyone has a role in keeping things running smoothly. People must eat and sleep every day. Children need to learn, and they need to play.

That's how I came to be standing in a gravel-covered lot the size of two baseball fields in Reynosa in April 2022. This was the space that would become Senda de Vida 2. Those high concrete walls had already been built and loomed above me, but there was little else. A small group of us, some of the asylum seekers and a group of volunteers from Solidarity Engineering, knelt around some plans laid out on the ground. We were looking at a sketch of the bare bones of the camp. Tents would fill most of the space, of course, but where would the kitchen go? Where would the toilets and showers go?

Those were important decisions, but the goal of *my* work in Mexico was to facilitate play. That could look like any number of things. I had already donated some Rigamajig and Rigamajig Jr. sets that were well used. My hope was they'd use Rigamajig as a foundational system for pop-up play and supplement it with other scrap materials from the area. Such flexible, open-ended kits could be very useful in a place marked by transitoriness and uncertainty. But the new camp that was under construction offered an opportunity: the chance to install a fixed playground with more options for climbing and hanging and locomotor play. Playgrounds mattered to the founders of Solidarity Engineering. They had once been part of another nonprofit but struck out on their own in order to prioritize play in the aid work they were doing.

But here, at Senda de Vida 2, where should the playground go? And what would they use to build it? Fortunately, among the asylum seekers, there were people with all kinds of useful expertise. One had formerly run public works in his town. Another was a civil engineer. These people would take ownership of the process, leading the project. I was there to help them think through the possibilities.

As is my way, I started by sketching. While I was kneeling there on the ground with pencil in hand, I noticed a young boy who was hanging around with us. He was maybe six or seven years old, and I could see that he had a long string attached to his belt loop. At the other end of the string, he had tied a small, circular magnet, shaped like a washer. He had been pulling this magnet along behind him as he walked through the gravel lot, collecting whatever small pieces of metal the magnet attracted. Bottle caps. Bolts. Ball bearings (those thrilled him). He was fishing, gravel-fishing. He was making play out of nothing.

We would do the same. In Spanish, they have an expression: *con cualquier cosa*. With whatever thing. Supplies in Reynosa were sparse, and much of what was there would be called into use for urgent purposes like housing. By necessity, the playground would need to be built with what was at hand, but I would have encouraged that approach anyway. It's fundamental to a playful mindset and to seeing the possibilities in what you have.

I had brought a stack of DIY playground books from the 1970s, including Jay Beckwith's *Build Your Own Playground!* and *Do It Yourself Playgrounds* by M. Paul Friedberg. These books and the others I had stuffed in my suitcase were all about using readily available materials and working with the community to design and build a playground. That's what I was suggesting in Reynosa: Use what you have. Look around at the materials that are naturally in the environment. Learn from the kids. *Con cualquier cosa.*

We can all learn to see possibility in what's around us. We do it all the time: Using a pencil to hold a bun of long hair in place. Wedging a shoe under a door to hold it open (mine is called the "doorshoe"). A friend has a stack of books to replace a broken leg of a cabinet. In high school I had a plastic fork jammed into the knob of my windshield wipers, to stop them from running constantly. Call it hacking, call it a quick fix. It requires we see things outside of their intended use and appropriate them for play. It's playful.

What did they already have in Reynosa? As I toured the area, I took note. They had 6-foot spools from cables, which could be partially buried, then become climbing structures. They had giant concrete cylinders left from an infrastructure project, which make wonderful shady forts and tunnels. There were plywood scraps with a myriad of possibilities—and cleaning them up and taking crates apart were good ways to get everybody involved. To turn those scraps into new shapes to build with, we assigned kids different tasks based on age. The six- through ten-year-olds got to draw shapes on the plywood pieces. Any shape will work! A group of eleven- to fifteen-year-olds put on leather gloves, and looking very serious about the work, cut out the shapes using a jigsaw. Anyone who wanted to join, including many adults who'd gathered out of curiosity, grabbed a paintbrush and added color to the new shapes.

I saw that when the work of the community related to play, it gave adults a sense of purpose. It engaged them. A carpenter could make a version of Rigamajig and expand on it twenty-fold based on the children's designs. People who had very little offered to donate parts. (*Oh, I can bring more wood from so and so.* Or *I can get the blades we need.*) I could feel them getting excited. They had an emotional response. The adults wanted to be involved in play. They wanted to be close to it.

Everybody benefits from play. That idea of pulling the whole community into the project ran through everything we did, and right to the discussion of where to site the fixed playground. Initially, the thinking was to put it on the edge of the camp near the kitchen, where mothers could keep an eye on their kids. There was an undeniable logic and convenience to that. But I suggested putting the playground smack in the middle of the camp. That would make the laughter and joy of play a central feature of the place—it would allow everyone to see play unfolding, even the many migrants who didn't have kids, or who had had to leave their children behind as they tried to make a better life for them. To walk past play, to hear it, to see it, is to remember that it is still happening. It's a sign of human perseverance. Play lifts us all.

In the end, the playground couldn't go directly in the middle of camp because of stormwater planning. But it did get strategically situated between two important areas—the kitchen/dining area and the laundry/bathrooms. Those were places that everyone in camp frequented. In previous camp designs, the kitchen and laundry were next to each other. By putting the playground between them, play became a fixture in everyone's daily routine. There was no way not to see it.

The local municipality has since gotten on board with play as a means of bringing people together, and we're working on a

16,500-square-foot play park. This will be the first of its kind—intended for Reynosa's local residents as well as the asylum seekers who live in Senda de Vida. If we can play together, we can live together.

THE HEALING POWER OF PLAY

Play was on display in other more specific ways at the camp. Together with a group called VOCES, which brings expressive therapies to the asylum seekers, Solidarity Engineering was running a makeshift school and community center in a local church, and they were using Rigamajig Jr. for STEAM learning projects with the kids. One of the children at the center was a young Haitian boy. Like my gravel fisherman, he was about six or seven, but he was not exploring the camp with the same comfort and zeal. In fact, this boy hadn't spoken a word since he arrived. He came to the center each day when it was time for "school," but he immediately tucked himself under a table and wouldn't come out until it was time to go. Then one day the volunteers placed some pieces of Rig Jr. on the floor just beyond his table. Just a few pieces of wood and the bolts that went with them. An invitation. After a little time had passed, the boy reached out a hand and took a few pieces and started putting them together. Later, he scooted out from underneath the table and started creating bigger things. The next day, as soon as he arrived at the church, he ran to the Rig Jr. pieces and started playing with them immediately. And then he started talking.

That story is a poignant example of the therapeutic power of play. The most famous psychoanalyst of them all, Sigmund Freud, was one of the first to recognize its impact. He said he used play in his practice because it allowed for freer self-expression, it allowed for wish fulfillment, and it helped patients work through traumatic events. In the century since Freud did that work, play therapy has become widely accepted. It is used mostly—but not only—with children. That makes sense because children don't always have the words to talk about their feelings or experiences, but they all play. "Play is as natural to children as breathing," wrote Charles Schaefer and Athena Drewes, two leading thinkers in the history of play therapy. "It is a universal expression of children, and it can transcend differences in ethnicity, language, or other aspects of culture."

Schaefer, a psychologist who died in 2020, is recognized as the father of play therapy, and his ideas on the power of play are inarguable. Play isn't just a medium for therapeutic change, he explained, it drives the change itself. He identified an impressive twenty ways that play therapy can change behavior. Broadly speaking, those therapeutic powers fall into four main categories: Play facilitates communication, it fosters emotional wellness, it enhances social relationships, and it increases personal strengths. These four categories in turn impact and are impacted by such vital elements as self-esteem, emotional regulation, empathy, attachment, stress management, learning, self-expression, and more. It's as if play emanates from deep within us and lights up the corners of our psyches.

"A person's play is an opening to that person's being," wrote psychiatrist Lenore Terr, an expert in using play therapy to work through traumatic events. The cure, Terr says, comes from first enacting play stories with feelings included, a process known as abreaction that allows children to release powerful emotions that have built up in response to whatever has happened. Second is context. Using play in a variety of contexts allows children to see problems from a new and broader perspective. And finally, there is correction. Play allows us to provide new endings, to retell the stories of the things that happen to us. After 9/11, therapists had young children build towers of blocks and crash planes into them as a way of mastering their fear.

With adults, too, play therapy serves as a way of working through trauma, especially trauma that lingers from early in life. Play therapy facilitates communication and interaction among groups. Therapists sometimes use play as an icebreaker. I read a moving story about a counselor working with survivors of domestic abuse. The counselor started every session having the women blow up balloons. Working in pairs, the women had to keep the balloons aloft. Without fail, the balloon game got the women laughing. It got them to feel like a team. It eased the mood and softened the ground for the hard work to come. Another form of play—role-playing—is a regular component of adult therapy. It allows the distance necessary to relate differently to one's experience. It also allows us to practice mindfulness and desired behaviors and ways of communicating.

Play can help with physical healing, too. A study of adults with Type 1 diabetes found those who played with their partners some part of each day reported better mood, better coping skills, and feeling more supported than those who didn't play. And in children hospitalized for cancer, play therapy was found to decrease pain after operations, improve behavior and attitude, and reduce anxiety. Laughter heals. In experiments that induce pain, watching comedy clips increases pain tolerance. And for people who suffer from chronic pain, humor and laughter are associated with improvements in their condition, such as reducing anxiety and stress.

In Mexico, however, I was reminded that play is not only therapeutic for individuals dealing with specific mental or physical problems. It can be broadly therapeutic for entire communities. It is a release, a refuge, a reminder that there is good in the world. It's akin to the benefits of being exposed to nature. Not everyone in a neighborhood must climb a tree (though I recommend it) to benefit from having a park full of trees nearby.

That's what I hope the residents of Senda de Vida get from play. I hope that individual children benefit as that little boy from Haiti did when he got to play with Rigamajig Jr. And I hope that the larger group benefits from the generative, hands-on creative play of Rigamajig—from building their own playground, from rediscovering the play within themselves, and from using what they have at hand to engage in it. Asylum seekers are in a situation that is untenably awful. The parents have no power. The kids have no agency. Everything is uncertain and vulnerable. For them to be able to impact the situation, to take a material and transform it—to take control and make something from nothing—that's big, that feels empowering. It's protecting space for play.

PLAY AT THE CENTER

There are places in the world where play is acknowledged as central, where it is not an afterthought or frivolity but is baked into the infrastructure of life and work, where opportunities to play abound because play is accepted, attended to, and appreciated.

It is one of the joys of my work that sometimes I get to spend time in such places. In March 2023, I was the keynote speaker at LEGO Education's annual employee meeting. I work with LEGO Group in a few capacities. The product side of the company makes the toys for kids (and adults) that you likely know well. LEGO Education strives to bring playful learning into the classroom. And the LEGO Foundation donates hundreds of millions of dollars a year to organizations worldwide to bring play and playful learning into different institutions. They are a strong advocate and thought leader in the space. It should come as no surprise that visiting LEGO's headquarters in Billund, Denmark, means stepping into a place that takes play seriously.

I was there for three days on that visit, not just giving my speech but participating in the workshops and discussions with the group. There were three hundred employees of LEGO Education from all over the world gathered to learn about new products, meet one another, and share experiences. They were also there to play. I was delighted to learn just how good at playing they were.

We met in a hall that had the vibe of a fancy school gymnasium but the A/V system of a 3-D movie theater. When I asked what they use the space for, I learned that the wooden floor opened to reveal a second light-up floor with customizable patterns, so the "court" could be designed as needed. My host, Andrew, has used it as both a disco (à la *Saturday Night Fever*) and a pickleball court. This hall lives within the "People House" section of the LEGO headquarters where families of employees gather, hang out, take ceramics and cooking classes, and use makerspace facilities, a gym, and music rooms. (Yes, there are LEGO bands.) There were several unclaimed children running around. I asked if the place served as day care and was reminded that I was in a country where socialism works. The implication being, to some extent, the children belong to everyone, and we're all looking out for them whether they are our own or not.

As a professional facilitator of play, it can be difficult for me to participate in organized play activities—somewhat like a chef going out to eat or a professional singer going to karaoke with friends. But it's a challenge that I appreciate and seek out, and when I do, I try to turn off my analytical, critical mind, ignore the fact that I'm wearing my professional drag, and be present to just play. There in the LEGO headquarters I trusted I was in good hands. One afternoon we found group numbers under our chairs and dispersed ourselves to piles of materials spread throughout the building. There were maybe sixty groups of four people, and each group was assigned a pile. We quickly began sorting the pieces, which were mostly train tracks. We were prompted to connect our track to that of the groups on either side of us so that a motorized train with a video camera caboose could travel through the entire space. Sounds simple enough, except that between us were stairs, a fireplace, sofas, a coffee bar, and more stairs. No one skipped a beat. My group dove in and started building—ours wouldn't just be a stretch of track, it would be the party-est stretch of track! *Let's use the Mindstorms (robotics) to give it movement. How can we add sound? What if there is a tunnel with a whirligig so the camera makes it spin?* For some reason we needed a tambourine. Twenty minutes in, I looked up from our section of track and saw close to 250 adults completely engaged in play. I wandered off with a few valuable pieces in hand to trade for an axle, and found myself just taking it all in. It felt familiar yet odd. I knew this feeling, one of being immersed in play with hundreds of my peers, but hadn't felt it so fully since I was a child on my school playground. The importance of what we were doing was undeniable.

Multiple experts in child development—Jean Piaget, Maria Montessori, Fred Rogers—are credited with promoting the idea that play is the work of the child. I'd found a place that takes it a step further, where play is the work of humans. It was a place that values collective play and built their headquarters for it, not so that employees work longer (as often happens with corporate childcare) but to make their lives more creative, more playful. While I was there, mine was, too.

What was so striking about the experience was that no one was self-consciously hanging back. No one was arguing over right and wrong ways to do it. Nobody was too cool to play. The leadership team didn't sneak off and answer emails while others played. The assistants didn't feel that the demands of their bosses rose above the demands of the train tracks. Participating in play was as important as whatever work projects were underway; it was as essential as whatever they *weren't* doing while they played.

This attitude is what we are missing in most of the world, and it is what we need. Not to run train tracks through our workplace necessarily, but to embrace the possibilities of our environment and of our creativity. To respect play as something to learn from and grow with, to see it as a means of fostering our well-being. And to remember that it is part of us, that it is wired into our brains. Some of those neural circuits that underpin our brains may have atrophied from disuse, but if we reengage with our playful instincts, we bring them back to life, nurture and strengthen them again. We know how to play; we just need to remember how to do it.

3

STAYING PLAYFUL

In 2016, a woman named Pamela Robinson was going through a difficult period. She was a forty-five-year-old stay-at-home mom living in a Chicago suburb. Her twenty-year marriage was ending, and her three children were growing up and moving away, leaving her feeling adrift and depressed. But at a neighbor's Memorial Day cookout, she was inspired to join a group of young people who were jumping double Dutch. Robinson easily fell in with the rhythm of the ropes. Jumping double Dutch was something she had done as a child, but rarely enjoyed as an adult. Yet, on that day in May, she found she was jumping with joy, literally. The brief respite from her troubles felt like the answer to a question she didn't know she had been asking. It was a sign that even if she couldn't fix everything that was wrong, she had the power to restore one thing that was missing in her life.

Robinson asked a friend, Catrina Dyer-Taylor, if she'd be willing to join her in playing outside sometimes, jumping double Dutch like they had when they were kids. "If that's what you need," Dyer-Taylor said, "then let's do it." By the time they met outside the local high school, ready to jump, the two had corralled three other women to join them. From those original five women playing together in their neighborhood, the 40+ Double Dutch Club has grown to more than ten thousand active members across the US and several other countries, according to *The New York Times*, where I first came across Robinson's story. They have a Facebook group that's five times larger. Once a year, in the summer, the group holds a National Play Date, a weekend full of outdoor fun and games. There is double Dutch, of course, but also Hula-Hoops, hopscotch, and other old-school activities.

Clearly, Robinson wasn't the only one who needed to put some play back into her life. Her story speaks to the yearning that so many adults feel to rediscover the pure and easy fun of childhood play, and the sense of imbalance we feel in our day-to-day existence. "A lot of women over 40 spend so much time taking care of everybody else," Robinson told the *Times*. "We are worried about our careers. We are just always focusing on other things other than ourselves."

When our lives are filled with to-do lists and responsibility, play doesn't feel like it belongs. Or it feels distant and unachievable, even if we see it out there beckoning. It's worth emphasizing that Robinson's determination to play and the eager response to it from her peers made the news. *The New York Times* took note and wrote about Robinson's club because it stood out as unusual and, therefore, newsworthy. Many other national news outlets agreed and picked up the story.

Because it is so rare to see adults fully embrace play, even in much more mundane ways than Robinson and her clubmates did, it can come as something of a shock when it happens. A friend still talks about the time she was walking her dog on a late-fall afternoon in a park in Brooklyn. It was an hour of the day when dogs were meant to be leashed, but the park was relatively empty, so my friend took a chance and unleashed her dog. He was only a year old and needed a good run multiple times a day to wear him out. They played fetch for a while, but then the dog was distracted by a quartet of thirty-somethings making their way across the grass. As he bounded over to them, my friend was afraid he would jump on them, that they might be afraid of dogs, or be indignant over her violation of park rules. She ran over, calling the dog back as she went, but she needn't have worried. As the dog rolled and pranced in front of the group, inviting them to play, the humans leapt into the canine fun and laughed with glee. And then, as my friend leashed the dog and pulled him away, one of the men turned to her and said, "Thank you for letting us share your dog's joy."

It was a lovely moment and a surprising one for my friend. But not for me. As a dog lover myself, I regularly accost other people's dogs in the street to play. When I walk away, I usually say, "Thank you for the love." I don't tell this story to say you have to be a dog lover to want to play—though it helps. I tell it to point out that play is a mindset, a filter through which we view everything that happens to us or around us. Do you see the dog's joy? Or do you see the violation of the rules? Encountering someone who sees joy when others do not can feel as rare and precious as discovering an especially beautiful shell on the beach.

LISTENING TO YOUR PLAY VOICE

I believe that so few of us are able to see the world in this way because a playful mindset is drummed out of us in our youth as we internalize the "adult-in-training" message and learn to not play. We devalue the input of our Play Voice and assume our Adult Voice is the authority, right about everything. I'm referring to the inner dialogue that rattles around in all our heads. The Adult Voice is the rational voice that tells you how to act. In this guise, it's sometimes on our side. It's protective in a way that ensures ongoing functionality. It helps us dress appropriately for interviews and remember to pay our rent. It tells us to contribute as a productive member of society and wants us to do things that are serious and practical, to restrain and control ourselves. But it can also be punitive and make you feel bad—it might echo the criticizing words of parents, teachers, bosses, and other figures in your past. I find my Adult Voice uptight and boring but without it, I wouldn't have made it through school, those years of training to be an adult. And when we're anxious or afraid, the Adult Voice is what we're likely to hear.

But we all also have a Play Voice. I think of my Play Voice, which is very loud, as the nemesis of my Adult Voice. My Play Voice is the one that's comfortable ignoring the rules that seem to govern civilized, adult behavior. When we were kids, our dominant internal voice was our Play Voice. We trusted it and followed its call. It was at the core of who we were. My Play Voice still calls on me to roll down that beautiful grassy slope or investigate the moldy compost bin. It wants to nudge a coworker in a meeting or pass a secret note containing a stupid joke. Most things my Play Voice wants to do are utterly pointless and that is exactly the point. Play can be disobedient. The more rules exist in a setting, the more likely I am to want to play there. When I enter an office of *serious*, my Play Voice immediately wants to shake it up. Other people's Play Voices may not be quite such troublemakers, but they can be powerful nonetheless, for the reminder they provide that play is always possible.

It would be reductive and somewhat silly to assume that we have only these two voices. We all have a chorus of internal voices. What's important is discerning which to listen to when. Most of us only listen to the Adult Voice, leaving our Play Voices defeated and sad. I imagine they would keep a diary at the end of the day of all the opportunities missed.

DIARY OF A DEJECTED PLAYVOICE

It was a grassy slope. What more could you want?

I regularly see and work with adults who don't come to play naturally—or maybe just have very loud Adult Voices. About ten years ago, I did my first play training with a group of public-school teachers in Detroit. Through the play advocacy nonprofit Kaboom!, General Motors had granted an entire school district with Rigamajig for their STEAM classrooms. I was there to support the teachers in using it for hands-on, playful learning in their school.

Initially, the teachers weren't thrilled. They started our session dubiously and not at all playful. They were already stretched thin by the demands of the job and skeptical that this new element would fit into their curriculum. They made it clear they were not interested in a bunch of parts and pieces strewn across the floor of their classrooms, another thing they would have to clean up.

But for the first twenty minutes of our time together, I reassured them I wasn't going to tell them how to do their jobs. Teaching is their craft, play is mine. Slowly they began to trust me and one another and to play with Rigamajig. They relaxed, their body language loosened up, they laughed, they told stories, they even engaged in some make-believe. Two teachers sat in chairs behind the control console for their spaceship and described how beautiful Mars looked that day. Midway through, one group had what can only be described as a laugh attack. All of them were buckled over guffawing, eyes watering, unable to speak or look at each other without it starting up again. A little bit of play went a long way to helping them remember what was wonderful about it. I was struck by the impact of the experience on them not just as teachers but as individuals.

BECOMING OUR UNIQUE SELVES

We come to elements of our identity through play when we are young. As a curious and active kid, I could usually be found in OshKosh overalls, shoeless, mucking around in the backyard. One typical day, when I was six, as my mother tells it, I stomped into the house from playing.

"Hey Mom, you need to pull up the roots in the yard," I exclaimed.

"Oh, do I? Why is that?" she replied.

"Because I keep stubbing my toes."

With that, I pointed down to my bare feet, caked in the red clay soil of the Sierra Nevada foothills. My clothes and fingernails were always stained with the stuff.

"Why don't you put shoes on?"

"I'm too busy playing!" Exasperated, and having lost patience with the exchange, I then stomped outside to get back to it. Or so my mother says.

I don't remember that specific exchange, but I do remember feeling the urgency of play. Whether it was clearing the rocks out of a fort I'd made in the woods or mastering a leap from one stump to another, it was important—too important for shoes, explanations, or the lumbering pace of adult priorities.

And I remember the glorious freedom of play. As a child of the '70s and '80s, I had an abundance of free time. If I was ever bored and thought to complain about it, Mom would look at me like my face was on fire. "What do you expect me to do about it?" she'd say. "Go outside!" That response helped me cultivate an independent streak. I made my own play. I was always into stuff, touching things, picking things up, turning things upside down to see what was underneath. Sometimes I did those things up in my favorite tree, noticing details, examining pine cones and bark and bugs. Sometimes I did those things on the ground, where I explored the pond down the street, poking around the muck, skipping stones, trying to stand on floating logs.

My sister's idea of a good time was not the same as mine. I tried endlessly to enlist her in my fort building or bicycle adventures, but that just wasn't her type of play. During summers spent with our dad, who lived by the ocean for much of my childhood, my sister Tisha would lie on the beach reading while I transferred my explorations to the waves and sand, digging and building and catching shore creatures and playing with dead stuff. To try to entice her to play with me, I'd delicately stack shells on her leg or shoulder, testing how completely she could ignore me, until the pile would collapse into her book, at which point she'd throw them at me along with a scornful look. One particularly questionable plea for attention involved a live sand crab tucked between the pages of her book—a gift for her to find later! She was not a fan of my efforts. One of my stepbrothers was more of a kindred spirit. We rode bikes, sometimes for miles, and built ramps with construction debris from homes being built nearby.

My style of play felt as natural to me as the outdoors I loved so much, and still does. As I grew up, however, I began to see that my play was somehow different from that of a lot of the other girls I knew. And not everyone was comfortable with that. They judged me. Reflected through the prism of society's expectations, my play looked wrong. And, therefore, so did I.

I was bumping up against—or slamming into—gender norms. No one thought it odd or inappropriate for my stepbrother to spend all day racing around on his bike having physical adventures, but they judged me for doing the same. I was often called a tomboy. The word implied I was an exception to the rule, not a normal girl, a construct that just reinforces the notion that there should be rules about childhood play.

There shouldn't be, of course, because there are reasons we gravitate to different types of play. Play serves many purposes when we're young. In addition to helping children develop social and physical skills, play is an expression of and a means to our developing selves. Looking back, I see that in my earliest years, a form of symbiosis was at work. My identity was being formed through my play and at the same time, my play was molded by my emerging identity. Such early play experiences help shape how we see ourselves in the social world. For most children, that vision of who we are and who we could be firms up in middle childhood as hobbies begin to develop. At that stage or age, many children start to gravitate toward sports or theater or robotics, and their play, and playmates, reflect those interests.

Whatever we do choose and how we then do it becomes a window into our personality. It reveals whether we are nervous or nervy, introverted or extroverted, a rule-follower or a rebel, and everything in between. Your friend group probably has a Tigger and an Eeyore. And you probably know someone who is always out and about at social gatherings and someone else who is usually curled up on the couch with a book or the television remote. Those differences in temperament emerge early and don't change all that much as we grow up. Perhaps you've heard of psychology's Big Five? Those are the five dimensions of personality—agreeableness, openness, extraversion, conscientiousness, and neuroticism. We all operate somewhere along a continuum for each dimension—for example, very open to experience or very resistant to change. The psychologist C. Robert Cloninger added an interesting layer to these ideas. He wrote that there are building blocks that contribute to human temperament: novelty-seeking, harm-avoidance, reward dependence, and persistence. You can see how relevant both the personality dimensions and Cloninger's building blocks might be in shaping the way we play as children and the way we as adults think of play. Play changes according to where we fall on these scales, depending on whether we look for new experiences or prefer familiarity (an adventurous traveler versus someone who returns to the same lake every vacation), whether we gravitate to physical play or prefer quieter, more internal ways of spending time (me compared to my sister).

Play also showcases our personal history and environment. My rural childhood was heavy on free play in the woods while my friends who grew up in cities were meeting up in public parks or playing jump rope on the sidewalk and playing in stairwells and elevators. They have skills I don't have and are comfortable in places where I feel like an alien. And vice versa.

As it did with me, all that individuality in play sometimes conflicts with cultural expectations, most obviously around gender. Social gender norms begin early with pink or blue announcements declaring "it's a girl" or "it's a boy." Those norms tell us how to behave as children and adults, and they police play. They dictate that girls are meant to play with dolls and boys with trucks, that girls have tea parties and boys have sword battles. Their influence extends into adulthood affecting who we are, how we live, what our friends and family look like.

Yet play is truly gender neutral. Gender itself can be playful! I love wigs and makeup and fake mustaches. And I'm adamant that all genders should be able to use them. From 1998 to 2002 I performed regularly in San Francisco clubs as a Drag King named Electro. With his well-applied mustache, sideburns, and chest hair, Electro was a very handsome man. But that wasn't interesting to me. I wanted to explore character and identity. While Electro's go-to persona was an '80s breakdancer, wearing parachute pants and using moves I'd learned in grade school, he took many other forms. These included the Sensi-taur (sensitive Centaur), who had articulated horse legs and mournfully sang Cat Stevens; a spaceship with sock puppets (the puppets sang the part of the astronaut in *Major Tom* and, as the spaceship, I sang the part of "ground control"); and a hot dog with a mustard yellow mustache and a gang of backup dancers who, for reasons I do not remember, had elaborate choreography involving Hula-Hoops. In drag, we can embody any number of ideas—about gender, character, or social norms. Whether or not there is a stage and audience, we can perform something or someone else for a time.

Biology does not dictate how anyone should play. The pink and blue toy aisles in any big-box store highlight just how far off track we've strayed in this territory. By the time we are adults, many of us have been fed a constant and ongoing stream of subtle and not-so-subtle signals about what styles and activities fit our gender or sexual identity.

If we let it, however, play allows exploration of self and identity and comfort in the in-betweens. One is no better or worse than the other. Toys that don't play into gender stereotypes or norms are liberating and afford freedom in play! Toys like Rigamajig can be figured out, undone, redone. They are not fixed, and they are not finished. Just like most people I know.

Adults don't have to be done growing, despite what we sometimes think. We can reinvent ourselves at various points in life and we can develop new habits and interests. Sometimes we want to run around and be physical and sometimes we want quiet contemplation. If we can do away with the need to classify by presumed identity, we also open new possibilities for the types of play we could access, enjoy, and grow from. We could play with a hammer and a tutu—maybe at the same time. We'd be liberated from narrow (and harmful) assumptions that dictate behavior and identity. Things like, *I'm an athlete, so I can't do the creative stuff.* Or *Because I'm an artist, I won't join a team sport.* We can try everything that speaks to us!

For both children and adults, play can encompass and amplify all the things that make us human: our sense of self and identity, our ability to connect and collaborate, and the complexity of our beings, environment, society, and world. This is why free play is so vital for adults. It's a version of play that allows us to let go in ways other kinds of play do not. Organized sports, for example, need rules. Free play does not. It frees us to let go of the concern about what is "sensible" or what's acceptable to others, and to focus more on what sounds right for us, what we need at that moment, what just sounds fun.

THE RUSH TO GROW UP

All too often, however, instead of letting go of "sensible," we let go of play. The shift away from play starts early. I blame puberty, which conspires with coolness to destroy play. During puberty we all become self-conscious—more aware and more concerned with what other people think of us. That shift is partly biological. Beginning around the age of ten, new levels of hormones surge through the bodies and brains of young people. Those hormones change what kids pay attention to and what they think matters. It's the beginning of a whole series of changes in the brain that unfold during adolescence and take until the midtwenties to complete. Those physiological changes are evolutionary and designed to encourage exploration and independence. They ultimately lead to making young people autonomous, productive members of society. Those chemical changes we experience also temporarily heighten emotions and make us hyperfocused on our social lives. That shouldn't necessarily mean that we have to give up being playful—in adolescence or in adulthood. But we do. It happens because cultural pressure compounds the instinct not to play. Our society delivers a verdict on what we think it's supposed to mean to become an adult. If play is the work of childhood, as Piaget once said, it follows that putting it away would be considered mature. This is a longstanding idea. The Greek words for *play* and *education* are both rooted in the word for *child*, implying that both should come to an end when childhood ends. As a result, we devalue play in adulthood. How surprising is it then that kids aspire to grow up rather than be present in the playfulness of childhood? It takes rare emotional maturity to push back against the message society sends.

On playgrounds around New York City, I see that shift in action among the preteens and teens who gravitate to hanging out around the basketball court and benches rather than the playground. Around age eleven is when we lose them. There are still activities that could be engaging for children that age on most playgrounds— like challenging climbing structures and rope courses, and high platforms where it's easy to congregate. But the visibility of playing is a problem. So is its adjacency to younger kids. It's not considered cool to play anymore, for fear of looking like a little kid. When talking to tweens about play, I frequently hear "that's baby stuff." In the tween years, young people are "aspirational teenagers." Everything is about looking older than you are. Far too many give up on play in adolescence without realizing they have a choice.

Between my first and second year of undergrad, I worked at a summer camp. I was the director of ceramics, and live-in counselor for a cabin full of eleven-year-old girls. They were right on the cusp of childhood while reaching for adulthood. Thanks to individual variation in development, half of them cared about boys and popularity, and half did not.

The camp had a tradition of secret cabin campouts. Unbeknownst to the powers-that-be (or maybe they just looked the other way), counselors would pick a night and take their campers out to a big meadow or the beach and let them sleep under the stars. To add to the adventure, these campouts usually involved joining forces with another cabin from the nearby boys' camp. Which cabins paired up was usually dictated by which counselors were hooking up with each other.

One afternoon, I came back to our cabin for some very welcome free time before we all went to dinner together. I found half of the girls inside modeling outfits and the others scattered around the outside—whittling or reading or crafting. It was odd, this division, and the group inside had a distinct mean-girl vibe. I had no interest in stoking the flame, so I flopped down inside on my cot and closed my eyes. Within five minutes, however, it was clear: We had drama. There were new crushes on two boys from different cabins. One boy who was thirteen—older and soooo cool. A few girls shared crushes on him. There was also talk of a popular older camper "with the coolest hair," and they were trying to emulate her style. I tuned out for a while, until I started to glean that they were buzzing about a possible campout. Usually, the campout invitations came through counselors, but it was obvious that a few of the girls were conspiring to make it happen. The volume lowered to whispers when the gossip turned to other girls in our cabin. The ones outside were the subject of some ire. But they were so harmless in their awkward bracelet-weaving. How had they pissed off these fashion plates? After a hushed comment about the dolls one girl had brought (but seemed to be hiding under her sleeping bag), I ditched pretending to be asleep and went outside to get another angle.

Just outside the cabin I found two of the other group of girls doing a dance routine while the rest were splayed across a picnic table focused on assorted crafts. I sat between a pair who were carving wooden spoons, a favorite early-evening activity. "Anyone want to tell me what's going on?" Eventually Nora, who I remember for her humor but who was not laughing in that moment, spilled the beans. Half of my campers wanted a coed campout and the other half did not. The group inside the cabin was deciding which boy cabin to invite based on which had the most crushes. They needed everyone to vote. But the girls outside the cabin had migrated outdoors to avoid the whole conversation. They neither had nor wanted crushes. They just wanted to goof around and make things with beads.

Over dinner and well into campfire that night, we discussed the dilemma as a group. I proposed compromises. A campout with an older girl cabin? No takers. A kayak adventure with a boys' cabin, then a campout with just us?! Ugh no. Midnight campfire with boys' cabin, no campout? No way. I was scrambling.

In the end, I remembered that our cabin was not in fact a democracy of eleven-year-olds, and, as the adult, I got to make the final decision. Being grown-up does have its advantages. We did the midnight kayak trip, and it was a huge success. We kayaked to a nearby beach, and at night, with phosphorescence, it felt otherworldly. We gathered wood and built a fire. After s'mores, the girls with crushes forgot they were mad at me and we all played. They danced on the beach, they chased each other into the water, and the distinct cliques finally dissolved. The girls who had been most adamant about not being immature were right in it. When they knew that nobody was watching, they were able to play together and connect again.

EMERGING ADULTHOOD

The process of learning to not play continues to unfold among college students, and as a university professor, I had a window into that phase of life, too. Psychologists now speak of this phase as "emerging adulthood" and consider it a distinct developmental period. It can be a time for trying on new identities, an opportunity to change how you were known or seen in high school while also holding on to the comforts of home you still enjoy— perhaps you stop using a childhood nickname but bring your teddy bear to the dorm room. Emerging adulthood is a space between childhood and adulthood that is somehow neither and both. On the one hand, people this age often look back fondly at being a kid and some feel this is their last chance to really play. But mostly, they look ahead to the phase of life when they need to begin to "act like a grown-up."

The tension shows up in decisions like what to study. Should I take this class that counts toward my major and might lead to a job? Or should I take this other class that sounds more appealing and fun, and that I'm really curious about? Usually, the voices of parents and advisors (i.e., Adult Voices) are ringing in the background. What are they prioritizing? How many of us who studied Art or English heard the question "What are you going to *do* with that degree?" The implication is that higher education is only in the service of a known profession. But the reality is that most emerging careers are jobs that didn't exist five to ten years ago. Three-quarters of college graduates don't end up with a job related to their major, and I don't think that's a bad thing. According to a 2017 report from the Institute of the Future, 85 percent of the jobs in 2030 have not been invented yet. We simply can't assume we know what people will need to know in the future in order to thrive.

More broadly speaking, educators and industry leaders agree that today's young people will need twenty-first-century skills to be healthy members of society with gainful employment and everything else that entails. Those skills include critical thinking, resilience, creativity, systems thinking, and empathy—most of which can be learned in English or art as well or better than in math or chemistry. And they can be learned in play. Play is a path to *all* of it. Yet after grade school, it rarely comes into the mix of strategies for helping young people develop.

All that said, adulthood brings undeniable changes. In her book *Your Turn: How to Be an Adult*, Julie Lythcott-Haims, a bestselling author and former dean at Stanford University, notes that twentieth-century psychologists established five markers of adulthood: finish your education, get a job, leave home, marry, and have children. Those are the traditional expectations anyway. The first phase of the transition means young adults usually move away from the safety net of family and home (if they are lucky enough to have a safe family), and they acquire increasing autonomy and independence. Parents are often surprised—and upset—to discover that colleges and universities do not automatically grant them access to information about how their child is doing, academically or otherwise. These parents are perhaps not ready for their children to be adults, even though society says they are. The upshot for late adolescents and early twenty-somethings is more responsibility for one's own self. In popular culture, we now call it *adulting*. The term screams chores and what some might perceive as potentially soul-crushing aspects of maturity: earning a living, paying bills, keeping your home and body clean, visiting the DMV. What doesn't the concept of "adulting" bring to mind? Jumping rope, midnight kayaking, or rolling down grassy slopes.

ADULTING

Once we are full-fledged adults, much about life changes. We are physically mature—as tall as we'll ever be. We are legally "of age"—able to drink, vote, go to war, make our own decisions about health care, nutrition, and everything else. A lot is expected of us. Relationships get more complex. As you take on a job and maybe pair up and start a family, the list of responsibilities grows, making it feel hard to prioritize play. Even though I don't have children, I run a company, I manage employees, I answer to clients, I feed and house myself and my dogs. I also care about and spend time with my friends and extended family. I have a lot on my plate. As you probably do, too.

I imagine that like me you don't have enough time to do all that you expect to. Time takes on different meaning in adulthood. It becomes a commodity, traded for money. We measure time. We block it out. We plan and schedule it. We hurry up more and slow down less. The immediacy of the internet and the fact that we carry our cell phones with us all the time means we are always reachable, always on. As a result, output and productivity become all-important. Everything we do has to serve a purpose, i.e., be functional. Even something like meditation sometimes gets done in the service of something else—*I am going to meditate so that I have a productive day. I'm going to the gym so that I look good. I am going to stay late at work and miss hanging out with my friends to show my dedication and maybe get a promotion someday.*

In childhood, caregivers create suspended reality that allows kids a safe space to play, to enjoy the blissful experience of being five. By the time we become our own caregivers, we feel reality come crashing down on us and we lose the muscle memory of playing. We shut down our play instincts as a survival mechanism.

I have a friend who feels this way. When I talk to her about play, she pushes back. "Play feels like a luxury," she says, "like something some people get to worry about, and others just can't. I have kids. I have a job. Now I'm supposed to make sure that I play, too? I am still catching up with the five fruits and vegetables thing." She couldn't see that play doesn't have to be something that replaces other things in her day. It can be part of the regularly scheduled activities. The way you take your kids to school can be playful. The way you fold your laundry can be playful. The way you conduct a meeting can be playful. It's not about doing more; it's about doing it differently. It's not about making yourself do something; it's about letting yourself do something. We don't have to suspend reality to play. Play doesn't exist only in conditions that are free of paying bills and complex relationships.

Back in the first half of the twentieth century, the reduction in child labor led to increasing amounts of free play. Kids were sent outside after school and not seen again until dinnertime. In my studio, I've got a book called *Street Play*. As the title suggests, it's a collection of photographs of children at play in the street taken between 1977 and 1980 by Martha Cooper. It features pictures of them rolling tires down the sidewalk and jumping on old mattresses. I could easily imagine a photograph of my taxi driver in Palm Springs and his young friends in this book, making do and having a blast with what they had in a vacant lot.

But toward the end of the last century, something shifted. More and more, adults began supervising children's time outside of school, which reduced the time those kids got to spend playing. Between 1981 and 1997, a team of sociologists asked parents to keep diaries recording how their children spent their time outside of school. In 1997, kids who were aged six to eight spent 18 percent more time in school, 145 percent more time doing schoolwork at home, 55 percent less time conversing with others, 168 percent more time running errands with parents, and 25 percent less time playing compared to their peers in 1981. In this study, playing included any kind of play—indoors and outdoors, board games to baseball—so it's fair to assume that free play took an even bigger hit. In 1997, the average child in this group spent a total of eleven hours a week playing. In a follow-up study, the same researchers found that these trends continued. Between 1997 and 2003, kids spent even more time on homework (an increase of 32 percent) and less time playing (a decrease of 7 percent). Those statistics are unlikely to have gotten better since.

Some of the children of the 1980s and 1990s are now parents themselves and they're not necessarily spending their days (and their time) any differently with their own children (or themselves). Several cultural trends make it even harder to push back. The seductiveness of screens, which have grown to fill far more of our time since those studies I just cited took place, is a piece of it, but only one piece of it. As a society we put increasing weight on school performance (the culture of childhood is also very visible in how we do school). We can debate the wider consequences of this, and I grant there are some legitimate reasons for it: It's a lot harder to earn a comfortable living in a blue-collar job these days, so education is seen as a path to prosperity. Around the world, we adults have gravitated toward what is known as "intensive parenting" as the secret to getting kids where we think they need to go. Intensive parenting is exactly what it sounds like: more oversight, more organized activities, more hovering like a helicopter, and less unstructured time, all of which takes a toll on parents as well as on children.

Growing parental fears about safety, in rural as well as urban areas, are another detriment to free play. Those fears increased so much so that when journalist Lenore Skenazy wrote a newspaper column in 2008 about letting her then nine-year-old son ride the New York City subway home alone, there was a media uproar. Skenazy stood her ground and went on to write the book *Free-Range Kids*. For the record, she believes in bike helmets, car seats, and many other forms of safety for kids. But she says, "I also believe our kids do not need a security detail every time they leave the house. Our kids are safer than we think and more competent, too. They deserve a chance to stretch and grow and do what we did—stay out until the streetlights come on." Nonetheless, Skenazy was quickly dubbed "America's Worst Mom."

We adults may not worry that much about our own safety— though sometimes we do—but we do seem to be engaged in what I'd call intensive adulting. It's as if we are hovering over our own shoulders. Our lives, too, are more crammed with organized activities and afford us fewer opportunities for unstructured time.

RETHINKING THE GOALS OF ADULTHOOD

Scientists and philosophers throughout time have considered the true purpose of adulthood and have come to different answers.

At a fundamental level, evolutionary biologists say the goal of being an adult is to survive, and to reproduce and pass your genes on to the next generation. They speak of a baboon "making a living" in the African savanna, and of course they don't mean this in human terms—that the monkey is earning enough money to pay rent and make car payments. They mean the baboon has to find enough food to serve its bodily energy requirements, enough food to live. They mean that baboons must help their young find enough food, too. They also must manage relationships with other animals and try to fend off lions and other predators. That is "making a living"—that is adulthood—at its most basic.

Philosophers who grapple with the capabilities of humans, not other animals, are less reductive. Socrates believed that adulthood meant the ability to think clearly, make reasoned decisions, and live a virtuous life. This type of reasoning concerns moral maturity, and the life of the mind. It amuses me, however, that Socrates enjoyed bucking the social norms of his day. The Ancient Greeks prized beauty—their sculptures have perfectly toned muscles, symmetrical features, and clothing draped just so, as if the subjects spent all day in the gym and had stylists on call. Socrates, however, disregarded his appearance completely, going around town barefoot and unwashed, hair long and unkempt, often wearing the clothes he had slept in. He already didn't fit in; why not go all the way into being different? That may have made it easier for him to think differently. He was never going to be like everyone else, so he wasn't constrained by the need to. He could even be a bit judgy with it. In his speech defending himself after being accused of corrupting the youth of Athens, he argued that his fellow Athenians cared too much for wealth, reputation, and their bodies. The goal of a human (adult) life, he argued, should be tending to the health of one's soul.

Friedrich Nietzsche also addressed the concept of adulthood: "The maturity of man—that means, to have reacquired the seriousness that one had as a child at play," he wrote in *Beyond Good and Evil*. I think he meant not that we should be serious, but that play is serious business and children know it. They give it their full attention. Nietzsche thought life was full of pain, and that play was the means of coping with that pain.

I especially like his description of the metamorphoses of the spirit, to which he ascribes three stages—using the metaphors of a camel, a lion, and a child (with a dragon thrown in as the bad guy). First, the spirit becomes a camel that kneels to take on a load—that's education and knowledge. Then, as the camel moves through the desert, it gets lonely and no longer wants to bear its burden. It morphs into a lion to free itself. Why a lion? Because a lion is strong enough to overthrow the dragon, the existing lord, who is the obstacle to freedom. Written on every one of the dragon's shiny scales are the words *Thou shalt*. The dragon represents all the institutions—from religion to your parents—telling you what to do and how to act. Thou shalt not giggle in meetings. Thou shalt eat your vegetables. The dragon represents the laws and rules of society. Once the lion kills the dragon, the lion becomes free. Upon achieving this freedom, the big, tawny beast turns into a child. "The child is innocence and forgetfulness, a new beginning, a game, a self-propelling wheel, a first motion, a sacred Yes," Nietzsche wrote. The child doesn't have to answer to the rules of society, the child is free. And what should the child do? Engage in creativity and play. Intensely.

It's useful to imagine ourselves as the camel, then the tawny lion and then the child again, free to play as we choose, free of "thou shalt." We don't have to forgo all the rules—or kill the dragon, so to speak. I'm here to help say a sacred yes to play.

I'd argue that the current state of human adulthood reflects some truth in all of the above ideas. Even though our daily lives can feel a little removed from the need to survive, as the baboons must, that is what we all are doing. We must feed ourselves and put a roof over our heads. The dragons are figurative but they're out there and we must contend with them. As individuals, we are also part of communities, societies, and nations. Those entities work better when we all contribute, when we keep in mind the greater good. Sometimes that requires us to take on some of the responsibilities written on that dragon's scales. But we also aim to be happy. And it's when we consider our happiness that rethinking the goal of adulthood can be so provocative and enlightening. Survival doesn't have to mean we work *all* the time.

I think of adulthood as a performance. We learn our lines and how to choose appropriate costumes throughout our years of education. We learn to care about how we're perceived. We learn to hold still, to make small talk. We strive to be disciplined and to meet our responsibilities. Gradually, this phase of life starts to feel more natural and less like an act we put on.

I say all that as someone who is acutely aware of the times when I'm performing adulthood. As a young adult, I was spectacularly uncertain about passing as a grown-up. In my first office job, I was self-conscious about whether I would look the part in my button-down shirt and work-appropriate shoes (or the closest I could come being that my budget limited me to the men's section of the thrift store). Looking back, I can see my experience of those years in the context of society's expectations. On the one hand, it was a time of adventure fueled by curiosity. On the other hand, I had no idea what I was doing or wanted to do with my life. The guidance office in my high school had a filing cabinet containing folders about different possible jobs. I pored over the files to try to imagine myself in any of the jobs I found inside them—accountant, secretary, veterinarian, doctor, nurse. Not one of them inspired or excited me. They were all so limiting. *These are the only things I can do? These are my only options?* We're encouraged to follow our passion, except that following your passion doesn't always line up with following the rules and norms of adulthood. We let people follow their interests within the boundaries of understandable jobs.

After some fits and starts in my twenties, I eventually found my way to design and then to designing for play. I created products and a company. I started giving talks and workshops about play. I became a professor. Thankfully, I made a path that wandered far from the options I'd found in the career-center filing cabinet. Yet I still sometimes feel as if I'm performing adulthood. My mother remains deeply worried that my messy hair will mean I won't be taken seriously. She still checks my fingernails for dirt. I sleep odd hours and sit in odd positions in meetings. During the pandemic, when all structure fell away and I became untethered from many of my responsibilities and from regularly interacting with other people, I became practically feral. I lived at my rural property in Rhode Island, which had no shortage of projects and things to tinker with outside. It also had lots of places to lose my phone for days. I once missed a meeting because the dogs and I had been sleeping outside in front of the bonfire and lost all sense of time. When I failed to show up once too often, my business manager came to check on me. He found me cheerfully rearranging the rocks in my brook so that its song had more bubble and less splash. It felt important at the time. And I still think it was important. It was what my spirit needed in that moment. This is all to say, I have never stopped playing, and never fully bought into the authority of my Adult Voice.

Play helped me cope in that difficult time. It can do that for all of us. Even in times of duress, play is there, a critical way of coping. We often think we shouldn't joke or laugh when we are sad, but laughing through the tears is often the best way to go. Play helps us manage "the shocks, angers, fears, disgust and sadness . . . we are doomed to encounter in everyday life," wrote the late educational psychologist Brian Sutton-Smith, a leading scholar of play. Two twentysomething young men I know recently lost their fifty-year-old mother. It was a shocking, untimely death. Immediately after the memorial reception in her honor, those brothers wanted to go play miniature golf with their cousins. They took comfort in being with people who knew what they were going through, and playing in the midst of the big, hard feelings was exactly what they needed in that moment.

QUESTIONING THE RULES

Accessing play requires an awareness of which rules of adulthood are important and which are not. If we articulate the unstated rules, it becomes easier to realize what's wrong with them. We can differentiate between the things we do because we think we have to and what is actually necessary. We can see which rules are based on a goal that feels relevant and which ones are not.

When I was a kid unloading groceries from the car, I'd always try to do it in one trip. My mom would yell, "Two trips, Cas!" But I thought that was too easy. Invariably, I'd end up dropping something and kicking it into the house. The other morning, I did it again. I tried to bring in the groceries in one trip. And I heard my Adult Voice saying, "Two trips, Cas!" as I kicked a twelve-pack of toilet paper into my apartment. But really, why not do it my way? I couldn't kick eggs or my precious avocados, but the toilet paper was no worse for wear after a few run-ins with my sneaker. I know I'm not alone in doing things the hard way. It makes the mundane more fun. Carrying groceries is boring because it's easy. But when I try to juggle extra bags, balance the paper towels on top, fumble keys from my teeth, then open the door with my foot and avoid the jumping dog, and barely reach the kitchen counter . . . BOOM! I won! The play is the challenge. Your Adult Voice might disagree, telling you to be careful and reasonable. Your Play Voice seeks to make it interesting, challenging, and fun.

At work, we might want to stand up and stretch every ten minutes in a meeting, but we think that's not allowed—even though movement keeps our brains energized. We avoid doodling on meeting notes—even though it feels good. We stay in the conference room when it's a beautiful day outside—even though sunlight perks us up and we could meet outdoors. Why not scrutinize some of the constructs we've agreed upon as rules? What to wear. How to socialize. When to eat.

DIARY OF A DEJECTED PLAYVOICE

The weird traffic pylons — so satisfyingly round and impossible to balance on. Why not try?

I'm not saying all rules are bad. During art school, I spent a summer in Rotterdam living with and working for an artist collective called Atelier Van Lieshout. Even by Dutch standards, the collective is a radical group. It attracts artists, anarchists, and makers from all over the world to work with them. One day, a group of us were biking somewhere and came to an intersection. Our light was red, but there were no cars coming, so I started to cross the street.

"Cas, what are you doing?" they said.

"But nobody's here," I replied.

"It doesn't matter. We don't do that." I was confused. Looking at my friends with their extensive tattoos, pierced faces, and Mad

Max bicycles, I thought they must be joking with me. Puzzled, I followed their lead. But once we settled into beers later that night, I brought it up. They explained: Rules like traffic laws are public courtesies, keeping things civilized and serving the greater good. My friends respect rules that are in the interest of the greater good, while rejecting those that govern social norms. Best reason to not jaywalk I've ever heard.

Sometimes the rule is that there are no rules. I spend some time each summer in the gay communities on Fire Island, off the coast of Long Island. The towns of Fire Island Pines and Cherry Grove are unique in the United States in that they were created and are governed by queer people. It's a community that prioritizes play. On the beaches there are no lifeguards and therefore no rules. As a result, people swim wherever and whenever they want, including at night. We dance on the beach. Dogs run free. Clothing is optional. When there are shark sightings, a volunteer puts out a flag and word travels down the beach. We take care of one another, and it creates the safety and freedom to play as we choose. The people in these communities are people who have questioned and rejected some of society's rules already, to live as we want to and to be ourselves. In the wider world, away from the beach, that makes us vulnerable. In this protected community, we trust we are safe.

Challenging rules can be a brave act (of course, kicking rolls of toilet paper is on a different end of the bravery spectrum than coming out as queer). Sometimes creating the conditions for free play means being brave. It requires an awareness of the interplay between vulnerability, trust, and risk. For adults, to let themselves play is to let themselves be vulnerable. It is taking a risk.

To do that, it helps to trust the people around you. When we're children, so long as we're being raised by loving adults, much of our vulnerability is physical. Risk looks like sharp objects, traffic, and leaping from tall places. As adults, risk looks like social rejection, endeavors at which we could fail, and the judgment of others. We have a lot of reasons to avoid all that. We've been hurt, heartbroken, disappointed. We've made mistakes, big and small. Who wants to repeat those experiences?

D. W. Winnicott wrote about the concept of "a holding environment." It begins literally with mothers holding their babies and giving them a sense of safety. In time, the holding space widens as we venture further from it, gaining confidence from the risk of leaving and the knowledge that we can return. As adults, our friends and coworkers are part of our holding space. If we trust them, we can be brave and take risks and know that we are safe. To play, freely, we make a conscious choice to be vulnerable, to open ourselves to potential dangers. We have to admit what we want and ask for it, whether that's to kindle a new friendship or to dance with a stranger. The rewards for that risk are wonder, connection, awe, learning, growth, and, yes, fun.

According to Indigenous scholar, teacher, and healer Eduardo Duran, who is a practicing clinical psychologist, trust is yours to give, not someone else's to earn. You decide who to trust, where, and when. What do you need to feel safe? Adult minds often emphasize safety in environments that pose very little risk. Are you overthinking the dangers? Are the rules you're following keeping you safe or just keeping you from playing? Are they worth questioning? Sometimes it's as simple as trusting yourself.

HOW WE PLAY

Adults do play. Of course we do. But we tend to have awfully narrow ideas about the possibilities. The same four things come up again and again when I talk to people about playing as an adult.

Sports. Video games. Booze. Sex.

Sure, there are exceptions. Activities like axe throwing and shuffleboard are popping up in strip malls. The continuing popularity of bowling and karaoke is encouraging because they are social games and people don't seem attached to being "good" at them. I love this about both activities—you shine by giving it your all, *especially* if you sing off-key or don't hit a single pin. The escape rooms that have proliferated around the country challenge our creativity and help us remember how to collaborate. And there was an adult coloring book trend for a while there, which gave people a chance to slow down, to occupy their hands and minds with meditative play.

Mostly, however, we rely on sports, video games, booze, and sex.

If you think video games are mostly for kids, you're very wrong. The average age of gamers is thirty-three and the video game industry claims that about two-thirds of adults play games, mostly on their smartphones. (That includes Wordle.) I make no judgments about this but want to point out that more time on your phone takes you away from in-person activities. It can be addictive. It's sedentary.

Sports are obviously not sedentary. Many adults love sports, and they keep playing competitively. I know a twentysomething man in Chicago who is part of three different adult leagues—

soccer, volleyball, basketball—plus rock climbs regularly with friends. Such activities provide exercise and social connection, and because they are regularly scheduled, they commit adults to getting away from work. Being accountable to others can help prioritize the play, making it harder to cancel or just not go.

But involvement in organized sports decreases dramatically as we age. In a 2015 national poll of more than 2,500 adults over eighteen, about 40 percent of the younger group (up to age twenty-five) were still playing sports, followed by a steep drop-off at twenty-six, and by the age of fifty and beyond, only 20 percent of adults still played sports. (Men are more than twice as likely as women to report playing sports as adults.) Interestingly, these same adults, if they are parents, cite wonderful benefits from sports for their children. They themselves, however, stop playing because of health problems, lack of interest, or inconvenience. I'd guess it also relates to decreasing ability. Can it be fun if we're no longer good at it? To be clear, older adults do continue to exercise—about half said they regularly walked or lifted weights. Just working out can be playful. For me, running is meditative play. But working out can often be as much about goals and extrinsic motivation as organized sports. It's about faster times and beating the competition or losing weight and keeping fit.

As for booze, it's hard not to notice that much of what adults do for fun is set up around drinking. After-work drinks are called happy hour. (All the hours before can't be happy?) We add alcohol (and other substances) to nearly every social event. It's the very definition of adult socializing. Studies show that young people are motivated to drink by the expectation that it will make it easier to mingle and have fun with friends. "And that, for them, outweighed any potential negative consequences," according to *The New York Times*. For middle-aged and older adults, booze is both a social lubricant and a way to deal with stress.

The need for alcohol to shed our inhibitions provides an important insight about what keeps us from playing. Think about what we do once alcohol has lifted our inhibitory filter. We often talk about embarrassing things we've done, people we love or have lost, our fears and our dreams. We divulge secrets and wander into the territory of the taboo. We show our emotions. We feel liberated in what emerges when we "cut loose." In the morning, however, we often feel ashamed of our behavior, and vow never to do that again. And yet, under the influence, we're freeing parts of ourselves that clearly long for expression. How can we feel safe enough in social settings to discover and share these things without alcohol? Could we give ourselves permission to socialize, linger, and relax without "liquid courage"?

If your Play Voice wants to go out and connect, and your Adult Voice is worried about work in the morning, let them collaborate on a plan for the night that is both playful and responsible. That's a skill I've worked on over the years. As a Leo, I tend toward eccentric, which means that in social situations I tend to go big. Now, before I go into a party or club, I take a beat and remind myself that I don't have to be the life of the party. I'm there to be with my friends, or dance with strangers, or listen to music, and be open to whatever the night might bring. I don't need to stay on the party train until the end of the line.

I practice this trust when there's no drinking involved, too. I do it by inviting people to play, which sometimes looks like striking up conversations with strangers. Recently, in the grocery store, I was standing in line behind a dad whose baby kept grabbing tiny $12 bottles of fancy lotion in the checkout lane. I started joking with the dad: "Oh sheesh, this one's got expensive taste already." He jumped in with something like, "Yeah, we've got quite a beauty regimen," and the riff kept going from there. But on other occasions, in response to my invitation to play, people send clear "Keep your dad-jokes to yourself, stranger" signals. No harm done, though. Not everyone will want to play, and you have to trust that it's worth taking the risk.

Sex, of course, is the most adult form of social connection. Sex can be about power, creativity, physical sensation, culture, taboo, and much more. As a highly personal yet very collaborative form of adult play, it has garnered countless books and an entire industry to its name. The Hebrew translation for sex is *yada*, which also means deep connection, to be known intimately. I love this because I think of sex as connected playing. Whether it's intimate and vulnerable or more casual, I'd argue it always affords a level of attention and mutual trust that doesn't come easily for most adults in their daily lives. That connection and ease of being tuned into another person is one we might remember from childhood play.

But, if these activities are all we think of when we think of Adult Play, we're boxing ourselves in. They are too limiting. What about all the other ways we can play? We do very little that counts as free play, like making time to lie under a tree to watch the sun play in the lacy patterns of the branches. All our games with rules don't count as free play. We don't embrace play the way children do and we don't cavort the way animals do. We acquire tools to *help* us cavort, such as surfboards, Jet Skis, Rollerblades, skateboards, and bikes. It's not an accident that flashy cars and boats, horses, and camping gear are often labeled "toys," a signifier of their luxury status. Acquiring such things is one version of adult play. It's play as a consumer experience. Notably, the car you use to get to work or take the kids to school is not called a toy. No one needs toys necessarily, even children. Dispensing with toys as a necessary condition of play reminds us that play is everywhere and that it comes from inside us. In an intriguing study in Germany, researchers experimented with a "toy-free kindergarten" for three months. At first the children were thrown, but teachers noticed that the children soon began talking more together and planning their play, especially when it incorporated the outdoors.

When I talk to adults in workshops and presentations, I have to specify "free play" and define it. Even when I define play at the outset of a talk, I still repeat the qualifier "free" as I talk because my audiences are so used to thinking about play as things like sports or video games. They've forgotten what else it is or can be. In some places, the very idea of free play is hard to talk about. I work extensively in both Italy and China, where my translators struggle to interpret the concept—in both languages the word for "play" means "game."

MAPPING THE WORLD OF ADULT PLAY

Remember the list of play types (rough and tumble play, imaginative play, etc.)? Play types have been developed to organize, understand, and help discuss children's play. They come from studying children at play and are influenced by how play functions for early stages in life, society, and human development. Adults play differently from children, based on where we are developmentally and socially. And we express our play in a variety of ways because we are individuals. Each of us will want to play according to the day, our mood, and our interests. To capture the full flavor of adult play, I think we need our own taxonomy of play. This is not to say there isn't commonality in play at all stages of life, but to understand how adults play, how we *can* play, we need a new lens and shared language.

In my years of working with adults and play, I've noticed some common threads that show up repeatedly. And you'll spot a few themes in the play types for adults that I propose below, but since they're in most everything, they aren't their own type. Many adult play types include some form of social connection. If you're like me, it usually doesn't matter what we're doing; the goal is to do it together. Whether it's fixing a bookshelf, grocery shopping, or going dancing, it's all quality time. Being with our friends, bonding in whatever circumstances we can find, is playful. "Friendship is a shortcut to play," says Tim Brown, the former CEO of design firm IDEO.

Play also commonly serves as a pressure release valve. It's a low-stakes way to let off steam, a way to grapple with emotions, to let go of cares and worries for a time. It helps us celebrate good times and cope with hard times. If we let go of our biases around good or bad emotions, we can be playful even when we are sad. Play gives you permission to feel joy alongside negativity, which is possibly when we need it most. Sometimes play involves challenging ourselves. It requires comfort with change, and it asks us to be brave, to put ourselves out there and trust we'll be seen. It requires trusting ourselves and each other.

In that spirit, I invite you to consider this taxonomy of adult play types. I hope it will help you to realize all the ways you already play and inspire you to find or try more.

PLAY TYPES FOR ADULTS

- **Meditative (Slow) Play:** Finding or creating order, or physically slowing down, as in yoga. Producing something with your hands that results in a designed object or completed thing. Something done correctly. Examples include building with LEGO bricks, assembling IKEA furniture, taking walks, following a recipe, doing dishes, arranging things, crafting with a kit, knitting, putting together jigsaw puzzles, and sorting things (Marie Kondo made tidying up into a form of play).

- **Creative Play:** Inspired creation. Expressing yourself through performance or exploring ideas through making something physical (or digital) without instructions, so the player makes some decisions and participates in designing something. Examples include tinkering, crafting, dancing at home, singing in the car or shower, decorating your house, doing makeup, cooking, creating art, and making videos for social media. (While this has the same name as a child play type, it manifests a little differently in adults.)

- **Problem-Solving Play:** Engaging in scenarios, games, or activities that require you to figure things out. Often, but not always, there is a straightforward goal or right answer.

Examples with a defined outcome include escape rooms, survivor games, word puzzles, and DIY solutions around the house. Open-ended examples include tinkering and rearranging a space for the sake of "changing it up."

- **Attention Play:** Noticing the world around you and engaging with it to imagine or understand it based on details. Examples include people watching, bird-watching, whale watching (watching anything but screens!), and making up stories to explain the details you see in the world. Everything's a clue.

- **Possibility Play:** Distraction or relief from reality. Playing with identity and world-building. Time spent in a world explicitly and intentionally separate from your work and family. Sometimes this kind of play never leaves the house. It might happen as we're getting ready to go out. Sometimes it is done socially, sometimes alone. Examples include the world of extreme fandom like sports fans who tailgate and wear face paint and chant in the stands. Or committed followers of bands, like Deadheads and the Beyhive. It also includes dress-up, drag, Comicon, Trekkies, Plushies, virtual worlds, and MMORPGs. Then there are Pinterest boards full of imagined lives and wish lists of Airbnb vacations we will never take.

- **Competitive Play:** Rules-based play. Usually against an opponent but can also be played to facilitate social connection. Also usually involves levels of mastery.

Examples include organized sports, video games, chess, board games, and axe throwing.

- **Embodied Play:** Using the body as a toy or as a means of exploring other things and ideas. Examples include dancing, sex, going to the gym, exercising, kickboxing, yoga, roller coasters, kayaking, trapeze, and all the other ways you can move your body.

- **(Mis)Behavior Play:** Playing with what is socially acceptable, pushing the boundaries of usual behavior. Examples include getting drunk, mischievous exploration, sex, playing pranks, snooping in your friend's medicine cabinet, sneaking into . . . anything.

Within each of these there is potential for free play.

We can use these play types to see and appreciate the complexity of play and to understand what lies at the heart of it. Hopefully, as you read those, you were adding to them and arguing with my examples. Is hiking embodied, meditative, or competitive? Depends on your mood! In Japan there are "Space Out" competitions where hundreds of people gather to daydream for ninety minutes. They dress up, freeze in place, and a winner is announced based on heart rate, theme, and stillness. I love this performative and completely silly rejection of productivity. It's misbehavior and meditative play done competitively.

These play types help us understand what we get out of the different ways we play, and they highlight what we might want to do more of. I hope they also illuminate ways of playing we hadn't considered or recognized as play.

Some of these types lend themselves to free play more than others. Some forms of meditative play and problem-solving play involve following instructions and have right and wrong answers; other forms are more freewheeling. Creative play is naturally freer and less rule-bound than competitive play, but have you ever found yourself in an elaborate game of horse? My friend Maria and I used to spend hours immersed in this basketball spin-off. We'd come up with the most complicated scenarios leading up to a shot which, if made, the other would have to re-create. Our efforts involved everything from somersaults to recitations of song lyrics to disrobing en route while lobbing the ball toward the hoop. The goal was not to make a basket, rather to make each other laugh until we couldn't stand up. It was undeniably competitive, creative free play. The basketball, the court at our public park, and the rules of the game all became ingredients we mixed up, redefined, and rejected as needed.

Our discomfort with adult free play was startlingly evident in a project I once assigned to a group of graduate and PhD students at the University of Southern Denmark in Kolding. This is another place that takes play seriously—they have a Design for Play department, where students will receive a PhD in Design for Play! I usually call the assignment "Playing Grown-Up." I tell participants to think of it as "creating an invitation to play" or "offering a hand to dance." Or maybe, I tell them, think of the assignment as the equivalent of a dog crouched in front of you, ball in its mouth, tail wagging. Their projects are meant to set the stage so that it's hard *not* to play.

The assignment instructions read: *Choose one play value that (in your observation) is inaccessible to adults. Design and pro-*

totype something to serve this need. This is a very open-ended prompt, so I added some constraints to help narrow their focus. That may sound counterintuitive: I want them to be creative yet I limit the possibilities. That's because too many possibilities can become distracting and even overwhelming. A constraint is something that intentionally limits choices and can end up making it easier to be creative. If I provide material constraints (e.g., *you can only use paper, tape, and colored pens*), students don't spend all their time deciding how to fabricate something elaborate. For clients, the constraints come in the form of a design brief: budget, deadline, the limits of the site.

For the assignment on adult play, asking students to create a play experience for a specific play value such as embodied play is a constraint. The play they design must also be playtest-able—meaning they must design it enough to actually see it in action. We'll use it and discuss how it went—like I did with the blocks at Liberty Science Center, where I made cardboard prototypes to see kids play. Often playtesting doesn't involve materials, or any physical bits, so it's the instructions and "play dynamics" that are tested and revised. Sometimes I ask that the project include bodily engagement and movement or that it encourage laughter.

The results are always intriguing. Once, the participants came up with a project titled "Silly Way." It promoted silliness with a deck of cards designed to bring the unexpected into a routine day. You'd pull a card every morning that prompted you to do something throughout the day. Possibility Play. The prompts ranged from "hop up and down while talking to strangers" to "wear mismatching clothes, and something backwards" to "make up an elaborate handshake with two people today."

Another time, a group created an elevator intervention wherein occupants had to sing in exchange for a ride, a toll of sorts, (Mis)behavior Play. Several projects have related to rearranging coworkers during meetings, finishing each other's work as an experiment in collaboration, Problem-Solving and Creative Play. A student in a wheelchair had everyone "lose a sense" for an hour of the workshop, Attention Play. Another called for a wearable whiteboard, so people had to draw on each other, Embodied Creative Play. Quite a few facilitated public goofiness—games created for bus stops, sidewalks, and parks.

Overall, I'd describe the results of the assignment as a response to taking oneself too seriously. When I've repeated the assignment all over the world, whether it be with students in college or high school, the projects are almost always interventions in otherwise humdrum parts of adults' daily lives. I ask them if they are playful in public, as they are prompting us to be in their designs. Usually, they are somewhat forlorn when they answer no. Why? Discussions get lively. When they stop to think about it, my students *do* know what's stopping them from playing. They want people to know they are smart and creative, and play isn't typically how that's demonstrated. They fear *not* being taken seriously. The suggested activities for adults then are about letting go of that fear and bringing a playful mindset to everyday moments. They are about infusing our routines—like commuting, or meeting, or laundry—with fun. That impulse is something we can practice and grow in ourselves. Understanding the connected and overlapping worlds of play that are possible for us helps us see how we can invite more into our lives. When we play, we don't just expand the acceptable territory for grown-ups; we expand our sense of who we are.

4

MAKING PLAY, NOT TOYS

I designed my first toy by accident. "Serendipity" is a better word because it ended up being such a happy accident. I was in art school, working toward a master of fine arts at Cranbrook Academy of Art outside Detroit. Cranbrook is an unusual place. A small and selective graduate art school, its classes are self-directed, with students spending most of the two-year program working in their own studios. There are no formal classes; rather, students and artists-in-residence come together weekly for critiques and reading groups. I was in the 3-D Design department with only fourteen other students. We followed our inspiration and chose collaborators, materials, and mediums as we saw fit.

I had arrived at Cranbrook at twenty-eight years old, having only recently decided that maybe I wanted to be a designer—or even recognized that one could have a career in design. When the question "What do you want to be when you grow up?" was introduced in the first grade, it stressed me out. Still does. Many of my students tell me they've always known they wanted to be a product designer (or a painter or an architect . . .) and I find that baffling. How do you know until you try *all the things*?

It took me two tries to get my college degree in feminist theory and fine art from the University of California, Santa Cruz. I had earned several scholarships on the strength of my essays and activities, and I lost that help after the second year because my grades were atrocious. I didn't know how to be in college. I had done well in high school because I was smart, but my classes weren't rigorous. When I arrived at college, I realized I did not have the skills to be successful in a more challenging academic environment. I existed in an endless loop of "Wait, what? I have to read this entire book by tomorrow?!" I didn't know how to do that, so I'd go play in the redwoods instead.

Between my first and second tries at my degree, I left school and went off to the Galápagos. There, I spent a year and a half as a research assistant to my uncle and aunt, who are herpetologists researching biodiversity (they study lizards). I was a quick learner and a hard worker. I caught more lizards than other assistants. I was a fairly good sailor, too. (We lived on a sailboat that we used to move between islands as the research required.) I was also very good at playing. I made a lot of local friends and was a regular at the makeshift dance club housed in one of the two village bars. The club stayed open until the town generator shut off around midnight or they ran out of beer, at which point, I'd have to talk someone into giving me a ride via pontoon boat back to our sailboat. But I was there to do science and my data was a mess. After a day of catching lizards, everyone else's data would be orderly and complete while mine would have elaborate diagrams and sketches of information I thought interesting but that was not part of the study. Try as I might, I just could not do something the same way twice.

Eventually I admitted that while my curiosity and love of the natural world could make me a great scientist, my aversion to data made me a terrible one. I returned to UCSC and ultimately got my degree in feminist theory and fine art sculpture. Then I had to decide what to do next. I had to figure out how to exist in the adult world.

During college, I worked as a breakfast cook and pastry chef. After graduating, I initially continued as a chef. I'd been working in kitchens since high school, which was creative work I was great at, but ultimately, I got sick of dealing with the drama in restaurants. Creatively I had other outlets. I was making art and performing as Electro, the break-dancing drag king.

To earn a living, I got a job at a high-end furniture company that specialized in Herman Miller office systems. I was tasked with proofreading floor plans to make sure the office furniture that was ordered by a client would actually fit in their space. I loved my coworkers, but the job was so boring . . . it left plenty of space for thinking about the art I was making or that night's performance. I assumed creativity was one of those things I would have to overcome to support myself. I'd been determined to be a productive member of society (read: adult) despite being a weirdo—making art, being queer, being playful. It took time to see that I could have value because of all those things. Ideally, that realization would have come when I was a child. I'm so grateful that the internet has exposed us all to the many ways we can exist in the world, and that young people faced with "What do you want to be when you grow up?" have infinitely more options than the filing cabinet full of jobs we dusted off for career day in my high school.

Once I finally figured out what I wanted to be—a designer—I was excited to learn how to do it, to take what I already knew about making art and hone my skills and add experience. For my first semester at Cranbrook, I continued making the kind of art I'd been making in San Francisco—kitschy furniture that included cast-resin toilet seats and lots of explorations of form and function. I loved the absurdity of there being handcrafted toilet seats. They were very beautiful, and they did sell to collectors at a San Francisco art gallery, which was thrilling. But at Cranbrook, at my end-of-year critique, one of the faculty members looked around and said, "I feel like I'm in the back of a thrift store." She was right. The studio visit went downhill from there.

From that critique and much reflection, I realized that kitsch was in my work because I liked the playful story it carried. As a designer, I want people to feel a connection with the objects I make. Relying on kitsch and nostalgia was easy. I was tweaking what I already knew. But easy is boring. By using familiar retro references, I was pointing to an existing story, rather than imagining a new one. It's harder to explore what we don't know, to start from scratch and write a new story.

New stories are often more interesting, and I hadn't moved halfway across the country to keep doing what I knew. So, when I returned for the second and final year of my program, I cleared out the kitsch, stripped my studio to bare walls, and started again. I had to trust that I could scrap what I'd been doing and get somewhere new. It was just me in there, playing with materials and ideas. I had drawing supplies and I had a table. I didn't know where I was going but I knew I had to get out of my comfort zone. It was unnerving and made me feel both vulnerable and alive.

Because of the time I spent in the Galápagos, I'd been thinking about evolution and mutation, about biodiversity and systems. From most perspectives, Herman Miller furniture and the Galápagos have nothing in common. Except they do. Systems furniture has tiny, seemingly inconsequential parts and pieces that are invisible by design. I'd find myself on a job site with a team of installers spending hours trying to redesign the space to compensate for one missing part. Remove one thing and the whole system collapses. In 1996, when I was in the Galápagos, the sea cucumber was being overfished and over the course of a year we watched as the whole ecosystem was thrown out of whack, ultimately impacting the sea iguana.

Experiences like that one remind me of the risks of seeing things in isolation and the need to understand things in context—by which I mean the systems they function within, their cultural significance and history, as well as how they are made, and why we need them. If you think about adulthood this way, you see it is part of a system, because it's part of the larger experience of being human. Your childhood, the habits you form, the environment you live in, your family and friends all help determine the texture of your life. All of those things and the social contract—whether or not you have bought into it entirely—influence how willing or able you are to play.

I keep context, history, and systems in mind when I design. In my daydreaming, I often play with ideas like these: What would have happened if no one ever invented the toothbrush? Maybe we'd let our teeth fall out, and we'd eat pureed food. There would be more innovation with blenders—pocket blenders! Maybe we'd have cool dentures we'd pick out in the morning the way we choose a shirt. Would we have dentists? How might things be different if we'd innovated sidewalks rather than cars?

I began that second year at Cranbrook by sketching around the idea of a playable wall. I was playing with patterns, cutting them out of paper and cardboard, drawing on them, using color in different ways, and pinning all of it up on the wall. The pin-up phase—where you get to really look at what you're doing and see what's working or not working—is a critical, inspiring part of any design project. Throw ideas and experiments and sketches at the wall and see what sticks.

The result of all that experimentation and thinking was an installation, a family of forms I called the Modular Ecosystem. It had both natural and industrial elements. Steel plates reminiscent of a cluster of limpets covered the floor and climbed 16 feet up the wall. Cushions upholstered in white leather attached to the plates with magnets, a parasite of sorts. They popped off the walls and topped stools extruding up from the floor, as if the steel plate had grown tall.

There was also a sculptural, skeletal curtain made of more

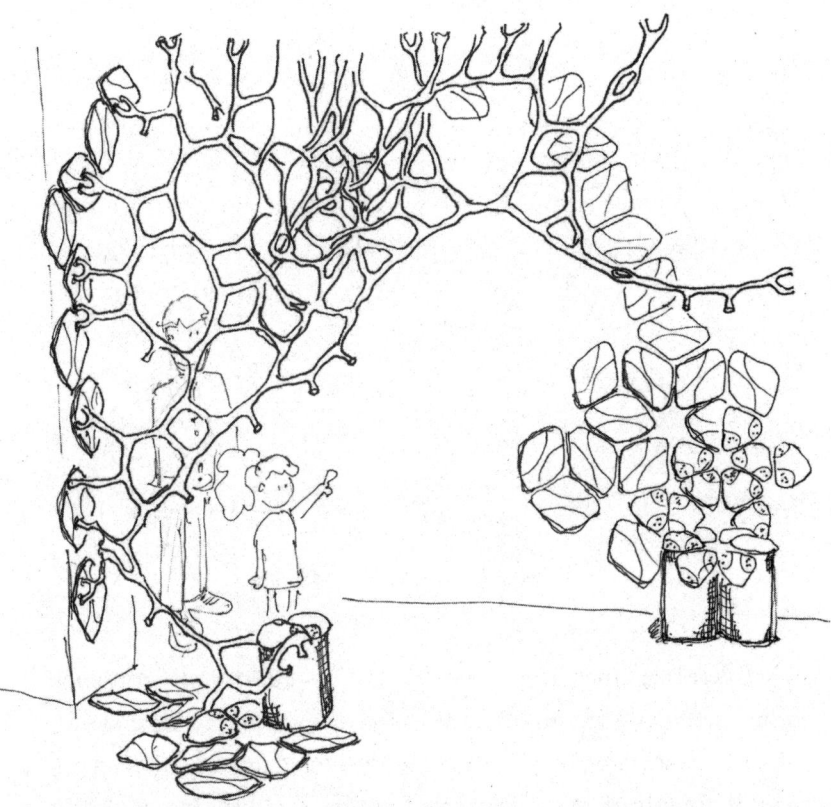

than three hundred flexible three-limbed pieces. Based on bone marrow and made of stretchy silicon, the pieces hung from the ceiling and the steel plates—and connected to each other—through magnets I had embedded into the end of each limb. Each piece could be disconnected and reattached in myriad ways. But the trick was that I didn't always line up the magnetic poles—some pieces snapped together, others repelled each other. Connecting them required some experimentation. I called that piece within the project Sprawl, for the gesture it made when all connected.

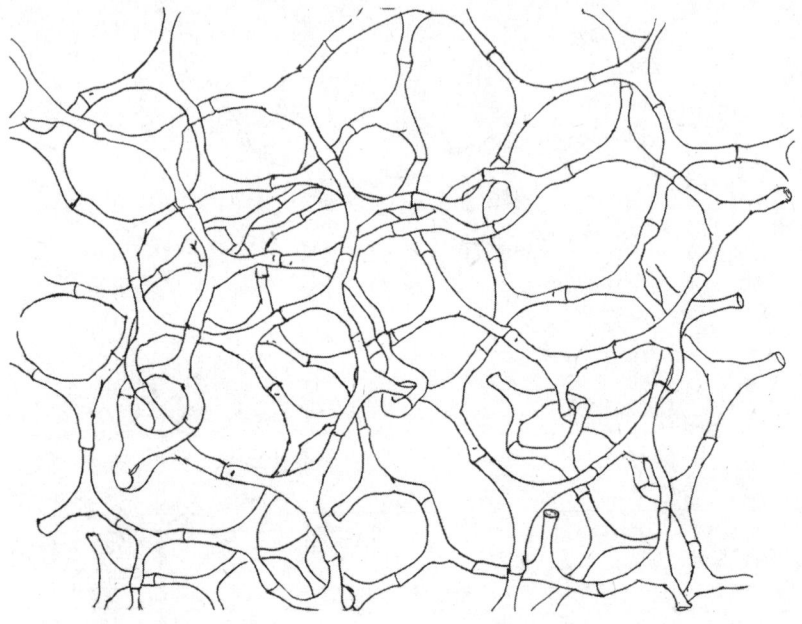

Taken together, the pieces of the installation fit into each other in a way they might have evolved to do—a codependency of sorts. As the concept and these designs came together in my studio, I realized that what I wanted from the sculpture wasn't just to evoke a story about what it was, but for people to play with the piece, to physically reconfigure, rearrange, sit, and lie down within it. I had my own imagined story of its origin, but how cool would it be to inspire people to come up with their own?

Unlike the previous year's work, this was a success. Installed in a corner of the Cranbrook Art Museum, the magnets in Sprawl—the skeletal curtain—clung to a metal grate in the ceiling. It looked like it had climbed there itself, slumping slightly under its own weight. But with the weight of three hundred silicone pieces, it didn't always stay. Every few days I'd hold my breath and go into the museum to find the whole sculpture on the ground like a pile of exhausted monsters who'd been partying all night. I spent a lot of time on a ladder that summer, begging them to stay put.

As a result, I got to listen in as visitors to the museum discussed what the work meant. They were playing and trying to understand it. They were imagining the story for themselves, inventing a tale, just as I'd hoped they would, of what it was and where it came from. I once heard someone say that it was some kind of mutation from a petri dish, which was much better than kitsch in the back of a thrift store!

Visitors seemed to find it as much fun as I did. One day I met a mother and her five-year-old daughter. The daughter had settled herself among the cushion-topped stools and was pulling apart the pieces of Sprawl and reattaching them around her torso. She'd made it wearable! Her mother was focused on a cluster climbing up the wall. I settled in to reattach some of the Sprawl that had migrated to the floor, and we all began talking. The daughter told me about her newly assembled body armor. The mother told me the whole thing was tremendous fun, but she was surprised that she and her daughter had different ideas of what it was or what to do with it. "Do we even know each other?" she said with a laugh. Sprawl had provoked a wonderful, elemental sort of play for them, and the mother had learned something about her daughter that she wouldn't have known without playing.

Sitting there playing with them, I had an epiphany: *What if I make Sprawl a toy?*

Until that moment, I hadn't given toys much thought. They didn't speak to me much as a child. Or rather, they spoke negatively.

From a very young age I was frustrated by the boy and girl sections in toy stores. I didn't want to play with the girl toys, which made me feel like I was somehow wrong. I did have some favorite toys—a stuffed Snoopy, a big loud Tonka truck—but my family didn't have expendable income, so I had very few store-bought toys. Thankfully, growing up in the woods, I had a childhood rich with play despite that (or maybe because of it). My memories are mostly just trees—that Ponderosa—and the river and rocks, my dog, swimming and being outside. For years I helped my stepdad while he played with his favorite toy—a dune buggy he built. When I was a young adult, before graduate school, toys weren't on my radar except as disappointing reminders of gender norms that used too much plastic. When friends of mine did have kids, we usually gave them old wooden toys. Or, since we were all artists, we tried to make them toys and help them make their own toys.

But watching people play with my sculpture made me think that toys didn't have to be so terrible. In a wave of clarity rivaled only by the moment in a romantic comedy when lovers realize they are meant to be together, I knew my calling. There is value in those moments I had in trees, but not all kids have access to abundant nature. There is value in helping kids make their own toys, but not everyone has an art studio or the capacity to make things. I realized there was a need for toys that inspire people. This matters. This is a thing I could do.

Designing toys felt as meaningful as what drew me to feminist studies in college and it would use my skills as an artist and maker. It was in my toolbox. I left my new friends—that mother and daughter—playing in the museum and went directly to the

Cranbrook library, which is a glorious, historied building filled with books related to art and design. The libraries of art institutions are the equivalent of church for artists, and that library was a religious experience for me. I started reading about early innovators in education like Maria Montessori and Friedrich Froebel and about the toys created at the famed Bauhaus design school, which included brightly colored blocks, a cradle, tops, and a chess set. As I pored over these brilliantly conceived, beautifully designed objects, I began to see a legacy of toy design, but I found nothing about contemporary toys.

I went back to my studio, booted up my computer, plugged in the ethernet cable, and searched the 2003 internet. I entered something like "designer toys" or "smart, interesting toys." My market research had begun. So had my education in how our culture thinks about toys . . . and play.

WHAT IS A TOY?

Toys and playthings have been with us for about as long as people have lived on Earth. Prehistoric dice have been found in every culture from the Aztecs to the Native Polynesians. The earliest examples were two-sided sticks, shells, or seeds and sometimes the two sides were painted or carved to differentiate them. Knucklebones, or astragals, also show up repeatedly. They were made from the anklebones of sheep, goats, and other hooved mammals and used by ancient Greeks, Indigenous Americans, and ancient Egyptians, probably for both games and gambling. An especially cool set of forty-nine gaming tokens—small, sculpted stones painted in green, red, blue, black, and white—was found in a five-hundred-year-old Bronze Age grave in southeast Turkey. Poker night would seem to have a long history.

Then there are the crumbling remains of stone amphitheaters that are everywhere in Greece, a reminder that the ancient Greeks invented theater, combining storytelling, music, and dancing to deliver cultural messages but also to entertain. That was play, too. Elsewhere, other forms of play were immortalized. In the ninth century, a trio of brothers working in the intellectual hotbed that was ancient Baghdad wrote and illustrated a compendium of mechanical inventions, some from the ancient Greeks and some of their own devising. They called it *The Book of Ingenious Devices* (a sequel was called *The Book of the Knowledge of Ingenious Mechanisms*). In his own book, *Wonderland: How Play Made the Modern World*, author Steven Johnson, who has made a career out of the study of innovation, described these early publications as compilations of fantastical inventions that included float valves, flow regulators, and water clocks, each an engineering breakthrough critical to the inner workings of later inventions like modern toilets and hydroelectric dams. But in Baghdad, most of these innovations were created just for fun—as parts of toys and playthings. They were the secret sauce in automated drumming machines and mechanical flute players and a peacock that dispensed water when you pulled its feathers. "Because play is often about breaking rules and experimenting with new conventions, it turns out to be the seedbed for many innovations that ultimately develop into much sturdier and more significant forms," Johnson wrote. His book is an argument for the history of play as an important space of "wonder and delight" where people were free to explore and create. "You will find the future wherever people are having the most fun."

Come to my studio and you'll see how I have fun. One of the first things you'll notice is the toy library. In fact, there are three libraries—toys, books, and materials. They are reference libraries more than lending libraries, and all are played with often. On a set of open, movable shelves, there are vintage wooden figures and building sets of all kinds, monster-making kits, push-scooters, and musical toys. These span interests, decades, and continents. I collect them when I travel, and from flea markets, garage sales, and eBay. My favorites are those that have been scribbled and drawn on, those that show their use. With time and agency, kids have personalized, improved, expanded them with crayons and imagination. I play with the toys when I'm casting around for a new idea. I take them out to playtest—like when I'm designing a toy with gears, and I want to see how other toys use gears—and I change what's on display according to my projects and curiosities of the moment.

It's only a little bit of a leap to say that something similar is true of toys over the years; they have shifted with the times, according to the thinking of the day. "Toys are like other human artifacts in that they lend themselves to multi-faceted human behavior," wrote Brian Sutton-Smith, the play scholar I mentioned earlier.

More than 150,000 of these toys spanning 300 years of play are housed at the Strong National Museum of Play in Rochester, New York, making the museum the largest repository of this form of material culture: toys as physical objects that are meaningful for what they tell us about our history, culture, and psychology. Importantly, toys don't just represent the material culture of children, but our ideas of childhood, and even adulthood. After all, adults have a lot of influence over whether and how children play, and of course, whether adults play themselves.

It's a central ambiguity of play, Sutton-Smith wrote, that "play is seen largely as what children do but not what adults do; why children play but adults only recreate; why play is said to be important for children's growth but is merely a diversion for adults." I'd argue, as Sutton-Smith essentially does, that those are semantic differences designed to make space for play in adulthood disguised as more "acceptable" behavior. He could plainly see the connections between "a child's make-believe, a mother's crossword puzzles and a father's endless rounds of golf."

Despite those ancient dice and knucklebones, modern toy manufacturing didn't begin until the eighteenth century. Scholars believe that, before "toys" as we know them were a thing, children were not treated all that differently from adults in terms of accommodations, and little was designed specifically with them in mind. Any community entertainment (i.e., play) was multigenerational. Kids played, of course, but mostly with household objects, or whatever their immediate environment provided—trees, walls, rocks, and so on. In Puritan times, play was condemned as sinful, with the only exception being festivals that provided a break from the rigors of work. By the nineteenth century, play had become a vehicle for education. As historian John Brewer put it, toys "became remorselessly didactic"—they were for teaching skills, moralizing, and imparting knowledge. The German education reformer Friedrich Froebel loosened that up a bit but still saw play as a key to learning. The innovative spheres, cylinders, and cubes Froebel designed inspired many of the building blocks and modular toys we still see in schools today (he also invented kindergarten). Culturally, we still toggle back and forth between these shifting perspectives on play—seeing it as positive or sinful (thanks to the Puritans), as primarily for learning or for frivolous fun.

It's clear upon arrival at the Strong Museum that this is a positive and fun institution. Even the architecture is playful—full of swooping lines and primary colors. Inside, there are clever exhibits celebrating play of all sorts. Traditional cases display everything from early wooden hoops and balls to video games. There are whole rooms of pinball machines, exhibits on comic book heroes and the adventures of reading. Barbie warrants her own display and a plaque entitled "Material Girl: Inside the Closet of America's Favorite Doll." It describes the way Barbie dolls shaped fashion but also kept up with cultural trends, shifting styles over the years. "Along the way," the plaque notes, "Mattel earned tidy profits on each tiny outfit." The Strong does not shy away from recognizing that toys are big business. In similar fashion, the backstory of Monopoly is on display. In 1904, a woman named Elizabeth Magie got a patent for The Landlord's Game, which she created "to teach players about societal inequities of wealth and land ownership." Others riffed on her creation, often calling it "monopoly." In 1933, an unemployed salesman named Charles Darrow played one of these copies. He loved it and started marketing and selling the capitalistic version we know today.

Up on the second floor of the museum, you'll find the National Toy Hall of Fame, which honors iconic toys as well as the people who made them. As you might expect, the list of enshrined toys is a catalog of popular playthings such as the Frisbee, the teddy bear, Crayola crayons, baseball cards, the Fisher-Price corn popper, Cabbage Patch Kids, and Nerf toys. Here the toys are sorted according to the types of play they inspire: make-believe, competition, creation, and so on.

Appropriately, the vast archive of Sutton-Smith's work is also housed at the Strong. Beginning in the 1950s, he studied toys and the larger question of play in groundbreaking ways, taking it all seriously while being thoroughly irreverent. His 2015 obituary in *The New York Times* called him the preeminent "scholar of what's fun." To the question, "Why study play?" Sutton-Smith memorably answered. "Life is crap and it's full of pain and suffering, and the only thing that makes it worth living—the only thing that makes it possible to get up and go on living—is play."

Once he started studying toys, it was obvious to Sutton-Smith that they were bigger than play. They had served multiple functions through history—both in adult ritual and in children's play. Dolls serve as stand-ins for people: princesses, people, soldiers (we invented "action figures" with the creation of G.I. Joe because we invented gender). Games encourage the marshaling of facts and the ability to make decisions. Since historians and social scientists were slow to take toys and play seriously, people rushed to fill the resulting void with opinion. As a result, our view of toys, Sutton-Smith wrote, "was more a matter of projection and prejudice than science."

He was right. How we let children play historically and what they played with reflected the prevailing cultural views of childhood and the fickle values of adults. The toys in my collection, for example, exemplify what we thought of children at various points in time. According to historians, the Erector Set, which first appeared in 1913, invented boyhood. "Hello boys!" it says, right on the box. The scaled-down (but functional!) replica of a printing press exemplifies a worker-in-training view we had. Most of the toys in my collection are building toys of all kinds—from plastic bulbs that connect with metal stems to boards upon which to construct a town and a story. The packaging of all of it reveals what we believed adults and parents wanted for their kids, as well as a larger cultural idea of how they should play. Sometimes toys are meant to occupy kids and keep them out of parents' hair, other times they serve to teach vocation (mini-cast iron sewing machines come to mind). Toys such as baby dolls (given to girls) and BB guns (given to boys) helped reinforce societal norms about gender.

In the 1960s and '70s, toys were the center of protests that reflected the upheaval in society at the time. The civil rights, antiwar, and feminist movements "brought their political concerns to Toyland, turning toys into vehicles for protest and reform," wrote historian Rob Goldberg in *Radical Play*. A group of parents launched a significant campaign against war toys—guns, soldiers, tanks, and so on. Others began to call for more diversity in dolls, the beginnings of representation of other races and ethnicities. With the creation of Black dolls, the "Black is Beautiful" slogan applied for the first time to toys. The sexualized, feminine appearance of dolls was also challenged. (The hugely successful 1972 album *Free to Be . . . You and Me* that took aim at gender stereotypes is another example of the way the politics of the era translated into popular culture.) "Toymakers were forced to publicly reckon with, perhaps for the first time, their status as entrepreneurs of ideology—as producers of values and not just products," Goldberg wrote. "Toys produced for children not only illustrate cultural change but also help shape it."

MAKING TOYS

When I started trying to make Sprawl into a toy, I discovered that many people in the toy industry didn't see things the way I did. They had a depressingly narrow view of what toys should be and, therefore, what play should be. The previous decades, with mass production techniques and all those television ads aimed directly at children, had helped create what Goldberg calls "a more uniform consumer culture of play." I was seeing the consequences.

I had renamed my toy Geemo. Sprawl worked as a name when there were hundreds of pieces but was less apt for a smaller set. "Geemo" was a play on GMO or genetically modified organism, which spoke to the origins of the project in mutation and evolution, and it seemed to better fit the stand-alone toy. (We ultimately sold the pieces in sets of five.) Plus, Geemo was unfamiliar—so the name didn't define its story—and the word was fun to say.

I talked to three separate toy companies about having them produce and sell Geemo. In each case, they were enthusiastic but then they would ask something like, when would I be adding the faces? Wait, what? I'd say in response. Apparently, they assumed I'd put faces on the ends of Geemo's limbs. And why is it all white? they asked. Because that leaves room for the player to imagine more stories about its identity, I'd say. Blank stares. But kids love color, they'd say. Sure. They also love ice cream but that doesn't mean you only give them ice cream. The toy executives didn't just want me to add color to the body of the pieces. They also wanted me to color-code the magnets according to positive and negative charge so that kids would know in advance which ones would attract and which would repel. Where is the fun in that? They were missing the point entirely.

People think children can't handle challenges, that toys should be easy. This is wrong. Easy is boring. Humans engage the unknown. Learning and play are in the challenge. I've watched kids play with cheap plastic toys and nine times out of ten, this is what happens: Excited by its newness, they make it do its trick; they look for what else there is to do with it and find nothing; they put it down and move on to something else. A really determined child might even break it open in order to make a boring toy interesting. The toy was designed to sell, not to engage a child through multiple levels of mastery, varying moods, and changing developmental needs over the course of months and years. Cheap disposable products don't help us develop a relationship with our things. We use them up rather than take care of them. Play becomes a thing to consume as if it's entertainment.

Looking back, I see that Geemo encapsulated much of what would become my ethos of play. It was open-ended, with no instructions and a fluid identity. It inspired curiosity and play in people regardless of age, gender, culture, or background. Making Geemo taught me to think about play, and the way I wanted children (or adults) to engage with the toy and go beyond it to imagine a story about what it could be. Geemo follows where imaginations lead. And it's fun. When kids are in the habit of inventing the identity of a toy, crafting a story that they didn't see in a movie or don't see in the world, that can be powerful. It's a license to assume that how things are isn't how they have to be, that at any point you can ask, "What if . . . ?" There's more room for empathy in this kind of play, too. I began to see the connection between imagination and empathy—you should be able to imagine someone else's point of view before you can try to empathize with it. Open-endedness leads to open-mindedness. As a designer, I can facilitate that process and that learning.

Through Geemo, I was creating play that was expansive. It could reach that five-year-old who made Geemo wearable but also her mother, who surprised herself by getting caught up in the pieces so thoroughly and developing her own vision of what it might be. My version of play was participatory. It invited engagement and experimentation (that's how you work out which magnets connect after all).

With trepidation, I launched my own company and started submitting Geemo to competitions, which is a good way to get noticed in the design world. One day I got a call from a representative of the Museum of Modern Art in New York City. They had spotted Geemo at one of those competitions, and they wanted to sell it in their gift shop and online. I thought I had it made! I was officially in the business of designing for play.

But there is a difference between thinking as a designer—those ideas I had about making good toys and what kind of play I wanted Geemo to inspire—and thinking as a toy business owner. The latter does not necessarily include operating with children and play value in mind. Mass-produced toys are designed largely by marketing teams according to price point, and what shelf they'll go on in the big-box stores. Licensing is a huge element of the industry, leveraging popular characters from video games, movies, books, and pop culture. You provide a story that children already know, and they're meant to reenact and pretend within it. What I was proposing when I met with those toy companies about making Geemo was antithetical to their entire business model.

MAKING PLAY

The deeper I got into the world of toys, the more I realized it wasn't just toys that needed rethinking. We needed to zoom further out and understand play. Designers typically approach play itself as something that's designed. A company produces a thing, and you play with it; you activate it, you use it. Too often, in the design process, things get closed off that could be left open. Play is—or can be—so much more than activating an object or consuming an experience. Good design should be about how the thing makes you feel, not the thing itself.

This is true of playgrounds as well as toys. As wonderful as they can be, playgrounds have contributed to our narrow thinking about play. In their design, there has been a historic tension between the needs of children and the concerns of adults, between conformity and creativity, standardization and innovation, risk and regulation. Playgrounds were created in part to keep children safe as society became increasingly urbanized and adults worried that the streets were no place to play. School recess, that cherished time when we poured outside, was a limited time in the day. Play now, but not later. And it was location specific. Play here, but not there. Traditional playgrounds draw lines around play and seem to dictate how to do it—swing here, slide there, hang upside down like this. That kind of design hems in our understanding of a playground and of play itself. It limits the possibilities.

Some visionaries did try to do it differently. The architectural playscapes of Japanese designer and sculptor Isamu Noguchi featured open-ended slopes and peaks and molded earthen forms, but only one was ever built in the United States (in Atlanta). The American architect Richard Dattner researched playground design by watching children play in the streets of New York City. His playgrounds for Central Park included pyramids, spheres, and tunnels for climbing in and through, and sand, gravel, and water to explore textures, but Dattner closed his practice in the 1980s because the liability risk of building playgrounds became too great.

The more typical playgrounds we see today grew out of the early-twentieth-century concept of the model playground, which featured the four S's: swings, seesaws, sandboxes, and slides, all made of steel. Merry-go-rounds or other twirling contraptions also frequently appeared, because what young person doesn't love getting dizzy and seeing stars while saying, "*Whooahh!*"?

Twirling until you're dizzy is awesome, but beyond that, our historically distorted approach to play—the here, not there mandate—is how we end up with unnecessary projects like playgrounds built next to a beach. Nothing makes me sadder. The beach is a playground all by itself even if there isn't always something to climb on. There is sand. There is water. There are shells and pebbles and maybe crabs and other creatures. A river, a junkyard, and my garage contain the same possibilities. A forest is a playground, too, one with limitless invitations to play. So much so that there are forest kindergartens around the world in which young children spend the entire day learning in the woods, in all weather—swinging in trees, making mud pies, carrying logs, learning to whittle and build fires. These kindergartens and other outdoor classrooms represent a radical rethinking of what school is and could be, one of very few paradigm shifts we have seen in education. Alas, they are hard to find.

A different approach to playgrounds—the one that speaks to me most—was born in Denmark in the 1940s when a landscape architect noticed that children seemed to prefer to play anywhere but the spaces he designed for them. (Just as children often play with the packaging that toys come in instead of the toys themselves.) Inspired by children playing in a construction site, that designer, Carl Theodor Sørensen, teamed up with an educator to try something new. They got rid of manufactured, rigid play structures and created the Emdrup Junk Playground. It was minimally landscaped to evoke the countryside with sections representing "the beach, the meadow, and the grove." There was a patch of grass and a sandbox and, yes, junk, in the form of scrap boards and other detritus. The sight of children using the junk to gleefully dig holes, build houses on stilts, and otherwise make up their own play drew international attention. The British landscape architect and early childhood advocate Marjory Allen, Baroness of Hurtwood, visited in 1946 and thought of doing something similar with bomb sites in London, where children were already building structures, lighting fires, and otherwise being creative with the rubble from the World War II Blitz.

Lady Allen became the leading advocate for what were eventually called adventure playgrounds, a name that went over better with local authorities than "junk playground" or "waste material playground" (briefly in the running). Lady Allen championed the way such playgrounds allowed for children's creativity and saw the value of there being some risk involved. "Better a broken bone than a broken spirit," she said.

The key is to understand playgrounds and toys as a means to an end. It's not about them as objects, it's about what they facilitate. That's why it's not a contradiction to say that I wish we were all just daydreaming or playing with sand at the beach as well as to acknowledge that I'm going to design spaces and objects—things that aren't always adventure playgrounds or sandpits—to help us play.

Play is part of our nonmaterial culture—an intangible like beliefs, values, and customs that shape behavior and social interactions. It's like our ceremonies and our body language, our traditions of shaking hands to greet each other in the United States but kissing both cheeks in Italy.

One of the great things about the Strong Museum is that in addition to all those toys, there is play on display, too. Kids run in and out of the giant playhouse. They play dress-up where a mirror and costumes have been provided. They send Matchbox cars racing down an oversized ramp.

Adult visitors play, too. They can be spotted getting competitive at side-by-side Space Invaders games and getting tangled up in Twister. It's one of the few places they feel free to let their Play Voice win out over their Adult Voice. At the Strong, Play

Voices rule. The setting makes it acceptable. Adults are invited to jump on giant motion-sensor gameboards and to design with the life-size Lite-Brite. A visit to the Strong goes a long way toward relocating that voice. Then you have to carry it outside with you and see where it takes you. There might be some version of its ideas that are liberating and important—and fun.

Nostalgia is also working its magic on the adults at the Strong, although nostalgia is a little complicated. Those "kidult toys" I mentioned are mostly collectibles, and they are primarily anchored in nostalgia. Play memories are powerful when they allow us to tap into a more playful state of mind. But romanticizing our own childhood play—and its toys—has limits in the ways it informs our adult play lives. How we played as kids isn't going to have the same impact if we replicate it exactly as adults. When I climb a tree today, it does not feel spiritual the way it did when I was eight. It feels lovely and fun. All my senses are happy and I'm proud of myself, but I don't want to hang out up there for an hour like I did when I was younger. Maybe you collect action figures or movie character figurines. Dolls are great if they remind you of good times and good feelings. But don't hold on to that as a measure of how playful you are now. You probably won't run around with a figurine and imagine it having adventures and tell stories about it while in the grocery store the way you once did. For one thing, you are in charge of feeding yourself now and, therefore, you have a different relationship with the grocery store.

Nostalgia works best if we remember what we enjoyed from our childhoods and adapt it to fit our lives as adults. Pamela

Robinson took something she loved as a kid—jumping rope—and added to it. She mixed outdoor games with social connection with women in the same stage of life. (As a happy by-product, many of them noted they were fitter after putting that kind of play back into their lives.)

Many adults collect toys from their childhood. Such collecting and reselling of things is largely about value, right? But something else might be at work, too. Metaphorically at least, when you put a toy on a shelf in a box, that memory and that play is protected, it's finished, it's pristine. Whether they are aware of it or not, adults may be trying to keep that memory safe. What if you crack that box open so that play comes to life again? You don't have to protect it. It gets to be with you. Play isn't a thing that's in a glossy box that you look at. It is safe to open the box. That memory won't disappear forever. If that toy gets lost, you'll have new play memories to make.

At the Strong, up in the Hall of Fame, there is an item that highlights this difference between toys and play. In and among the mostly commercial toys is something the museum has dubbed "The Greatest Toy Never Sold": a cardboard box. It was added to the Hall of Fame in 2005 along with Candy Land and the jack-in-the-box. The year the cardboard box was inducted, the museum's chief curator, Christopher Bensch, gave interviews to national media explaining the choice. Each inductee must have stood the test of time, entrancing multiple generations. The cardboard box is just such an item, he said. Since the modern version was perfected in the late 1800s, revolutionizing shipping and storage, children have gravitated to it, seeing it as an open invitation to play. Boxes are "rescued" for pretend play. They can become dioramas, doll's houses, cars, or spaceships. A box is a blank canvas. It's not precious. You can't break it or mess it up.

"It's a relief to know that there are great toys out there that don't require batteries, wires, power supply, and that you can power just by imagination," Bensch told National Public Radio. And in what sounded like it might have been a play memory of his own, he described the enduring popularity of a particular kind of box. "Word went out over the kid network as soon as somebody in the neighborhood had an appliance delivered to their home because we all wanted to get in on that refrigerator box, that washer box, that electric range box that was so much fun to imagine what it could be." Fort, anyone?

The inclusion of the cardboard box in the Hall of Fame is genius and represents play in the broadest possible sense. It celebrates free play, imagination, and creativity. It's a physical stand-in for a playful mindset. In the years since the box's big moment, the Strong has added the stick (2008) and the blanket (2011)—two more "toys" that are simply everyday objects that have been repurposed for play since . . . well, since the first knucklebones were tossed into other bones just for the fun of hearing the noise they made. Bang!

The playful mindset is in us and with us and always has been. We need to trust those instincts and trust ourselves. As we reach adulthood, we stop seeing boxes as anything other than something to break down for recycling, another chore. The goal of my work is to nudge us off the linear path sometimes, to inspire us to see the fort in the box, if only for a few minutes.

In Part Two of this book, I will show you how to think about play with the same fresh perspective I had to bring to my studio that second year at Cranbrook. I know it can be hard to recognize old habits and to make changes in your life. I'm going to help you do it. We will strip the walls of your mental studio and shake up your idea of what play is and can be. Think of it as looking for that nondescript box in among the Barbies and baseball cards of your life. Play is not what we have but what we see in what we have.

part two

the
playful
mindset

5

EMBRACE POSSIBILITY

My friend Shaka (who uses *they* pronouns) does yoga at the airport. They find a quiet, empty boarding area, sit down, and begin to work through vinyasas. On a recent trip, their idea caught on. "I wasn't paying attention to anyone noticing me, but someone approached and asked to join. We silently stretched for fifteen minutes," they marveled. Then as Shaka was gathering their stuff to head to their flight, two more people came up. "They thanked us! They were going to use the spot to do the same. Somehow, we broke the airport yoga seal." Shaka had given those people permission to do what their Adult Voices told them not to.

There is no rule against doing yoga in airports, of course. It's just that nobody does. In fact, when Shaka told a group of us about it at dinner one night, I was struck by the confessional nature of their tone. "I don't know why it feels embarrassing to admit!" Shaka said. I know why. Shaka did something adults rarely do; they let their Play Voice take over. Where others saw that empty gate as simply *not their gate* or as dead space, or possibly as a place to make a private phone call, Shaka saw room to move their body, to relax, to ease the stress of travel for a few minutes, to engage in a form of play. And when they did, they got the added joy of igniting a mini-rebellion among their fellow travelers, of helping others see an unexpected possibility in an airport concourse.

DIARY OF A DEJECTED PLAYVOICE

The sun felt so good on your face, still you would not lay on the bench.

Embracing such possibilities is the starting point for free play for adults. It's a doorway. Cross that threshold and you recognize that there are alternatives to our routines and many of our rules, written and unwritten. There could be a different way, place, time, or location to do something you traditionally do only one way, one place, one time. To embrace possibility is to pose a question you'd like to answer, find a path you'd like to pursue, or simply explore something enticing. To tune into what we need and to say, *Hey, I feel out of sorts, maybe stretching would help. I think there's enough space for a downward facing dog over there.*

Embracing possibility requires two things: First, that you start with an open mind. It helps to bring a little childlike wonder into your worldview. Kids would have no problem seeing the potential play space in an empty airport gate. Second, that open mind needs to extend to the results of your exploration. You need to be willing to consider a variety of outcomes. You let curiosity and a positive outlook on possibility guide you. It's the equivalent of choosing "avoid highways" on the GPS just to see where it takes you. The trip will almost certainly take longer but it could be an adventure.

THE WORLD IS A PLAYGROUND

When we enter a playground, we assume everything is playable. Let's apply that lens to everything else in our lives. How we play when we are young lays the foundations for how we play when we are older. Open-ended play creates comfort with uncertainty. It is the embodiment of constructivist learning in which children and adults (because we are never done learning) learn by doing, by actively interacting with the world, by experimenting and reflecting. "Knowledge, to a constructivist, is not merely a commodity to be transmitted—delivered at one end, encoded, retained, and re-applied at the other—but an experience to be actively built," wrote developmental psychologist Edith Ackermann of the MIT Media Lab. "Similarly, the world is not just sitting out there waiting to be uncovered but gets progressively shaped and formed through people's interactions/transactions."

If we become accustomed to open-ended play as children, we are more likely to see broader possibilities around us when we are older. We're more likely to treat life as the playground it is, to approach it with curious anticipation, looking for fun, for movement, for release of energy, for exploration, for social engagement. If we didn't get open-ended play as kids, we may have to work harder to polish the lens through which we see the world. But it can be done, because after all, play is in us.

Taking a closer look at adventure playgrounds is a good way to loosen up our play muscles. Adventure playgrounds are the epitome of embracing possibility, of looking at your surroundings and the objects there with new perspective. They allow us to see alternative uses for everyday objects and activities. They are about finding what you need in what you already have. It's difficult to describe what happens on any given day in one of these playgrounds because to adult eyes—that is, from the typical adult perspective—it often looks like nothing. I visited The Yard recently, a self-described Junk Playground on Governors Island in NYC, and saw a not-at-all-surprising assortment of play. One pair of kids who were around six were planting some herbs. Another group of slightly older kids was trying to hoist a large, empty plastic spool up onto a platform that looked to have been built sideways but was supporting them without fail. They explained that they wanted to put the spool under the tidy stack of tires they were fumbling around. Why? Why not! If a child needs a challenge, they create it. If they need peace, they find a spot for it. Playgrounds like this are a mindset as much as a place.

Adopt that kind of mindset and you loosen the strictures adulthood imposes on play. Any object could become a source of fun—an umbrella keeps you dry *and* it helps you channel Gene Kelly and dance; a whiteboard in the office lists the day's agenda *and* provides space for ongoing anonymous games of tic-tac-toe, or doodles that evolve as passersby add to them. Any environment can be a place to play—and you don't need toys to do it. Using what's around you in novel ways can not only save you from buying more stuff but make for a fun hacking project. Embrace imperfection and let yourself be creative with what you have on hand. Games like "I Spy" aren't just for car trips; why not play them in the kitchen or looking out your office window? Or you could pick a place in your town or city that you've never visited and just go to see what's there—make it an adventure. Usually drive? Try biking. Maybe you meander your way there, following the turns that look most interesting rather than taking the most direct route.

Adventure playgrounds also introduced the job of playworker, the adults who staff playgrounds and create the conditions for free play. Being a playworker is a trained, skilled profession in the UK. Playworkers facilitate possibilities—they bring objects into the space (ladders, crates, someone's abandoned rowboat . . .) or curate what's offered by neighbors. They keep an eye on whether anything in the playground has gotten dangerous. Because they work in a community and see the same children repeatedly, playworkers know who's who and what is likely to interest which child. By creating a safe space for exploration, playworkers become stand-ins for D. W. Winnicott's "good enough" parents—there to give permission when needed ("Yes, you can do whatever you want here") and monitor safety, but otherwise intentionally staying in the background. When kids need nails to build something, they collect old, bent nails and trade them for straight ones with the playworkers. (The playworkers spend a lot of time straightening nails for reuse.) This also means kids are always on the lookout for nails, a potential hazard transformed into an Easter egg. Playworkers are the ultimate play provocateurs.

It would be wonderful if we each had a playworker lurking in the background of our lives, quietly pointing out new possibilities. I am serving as a playworker in this book, getting you started. But once you hone your own sensibilities, polish that new lens on the world, and develop your playful mindset, there's no reason you cannot be your own playworker—your Play Voice will guide you.

Rich and joyous as they are, adventure playgrounds are usually not much to look at. They are full of odds and ends—tires, mannequins, scrapwood, and plastic tubing. And grown-ups, especially, have a hard time seeing past the mess. "To the adult eye [adventure playgrounds] are chaotic and ugly," said one commentary, but to children, they are "just possibilities." What curious human doesn't want to play in a pile of junk? It's an invitation, the beginning of a project to discover. Inspect me. Rebuild me. Start over and build something else. You can't mess it up! In the playground, the junk becomes loose parts that allow for open-ended play, letting kids design the play and the play space, together, and then redesign it the next day. Such playgrounds promote collaboration with friends and strangers, but also the ability to create forts for hiding out alone when the need strikes. Children build what they need.

The lesson for us big people is that if we overdesign our surroundings or the objects that shape our thinking, we make it harder to behave differently. We dictate too much. If we step back, we can see other possibilities. Very occasionally, I stumble on someone doing pull-ups on the scaffolding near my Brooklyn apartment. Because we exercise in gyms, that's an unusual sight but it thrills me every time—like Shaka commandeering an empty gate, I see it as treating the city as a playground. I felt the same way when I read about newlyweds in New York City who held their wedding reception on a subway car—it was a cheap way to have enough space for all their family and friends to celebrate with them. They brought decorations and food and music and had a party. It was hard not to see the subway in a new light after that story made the papers. Other couples have followed their example. And what a bonus for the strangers who happen to be commuting during the weddings—they get cake! This is embracing *all* the possibilities.

THINK SIDEWAYS

Early in my career I was asked to help reimagine what a playground could be. I was working at Rockwell Group, an architecture and design firm in New York City. The founder, David Rockwell, had young children and had spent enough time in playgrounds to think they could be way more interesting. I threw myself into the project with enthusiasm and what I now recognize was a good bit of naivete. *Why* are *playgrounds all the same?*

Why is this the only thing they can be? Why is everything attached to the ground? What if kids could design playgrounds themselves, through playing? I went into it determined to be expansive in my vision of a playground.

To do that, I needed to use the power of design thinking, which is inherently playful. Design thinking brings together what is desirable for humans with what is technologically feasible and economically viable. I am borrowing the definition for design thinking from Tim Brown, the former CEO of IDEO, a leading design firm that helped popularize the concept of design thinking decades ago. Thinking like a designer involves considering all possibilities. "We adopt a 'beginner's mind set' with the intent to remain open and curious, to assume nothing, and to see ambiguity as opportunity," the folks at IDEO say.

At every step in the playground conversation, people would offer suggestions, and I would ask, "What does that *look* like?" I was using my expertise to translate each idea into a form and an interaction. I gave the conversation tangible examples that then gave us something new to consider and debate. How does this design change what's happening? How does that idea change the opportunities for children to explore or to feel good about making something? It was iterative brainstorming. I was constantly questioning. When the goal was for kids to connect with nature but not touch it (due to the large number of kids passing through), I suggested a platform they could lie on to see up into the treetops. When the goal was an activity that allowed kids to practice impulse control, I riffed on hopscotch, a classic exercise in controlling movement. If we wanted to support emotion regulation, we could use loose parts that need to be shared, a way to practice negotiating over resources. If we wanted kids to explore balance, I'd suggest a rope course with balls they could clamber over. Imagining the unlimited alternatives for each of these is play for me.

There's no reason such an approach should be limited to designers. We can all apply it to nearly every aspect of our lives. But perhaps thinking this way comes more naturally to designers than to people in other professions, who are often rewarded for taking a more linear approach to finding solutions and moving projects forward quickly. Design thinking can mean going slowly and even moving sideways for a bit. That's because the sideways view of a problem prompts new perspectives. It is where innovative solutions arise. Sliding in sideways requires a willingness to see a problem as an opportunity, to tolerate discomfort, and allow for what John Cleese calls more "pondering time." Play is in the "what if . . . "

What if you looked at your life sideways? What would you see? Design thinking means reframing problems and that means reframing questions. Instead of asking "What do I want to be when I grow up?" or "When can I quit this job?" you could ask, "What kind of person do I want to be?" or "What do I enjoy doing?" For me, that was making things, building things. *What's a job centered on those things?* I wondered. What if we take the very problem we have been confronting—that adults don't set up their lives for the conditions of play to arise—and tackle it sideways. We've established some of the reasons adults do that—we are trained to strive to be productive and goal-oriented; we are afraid of looking foolish. What would it look like to tear down those barriers? What would it look like to do it differently? Embracing possibilities is a place to start.

Consider the wholesale change to our work lives that the pandemic brought about. We changed by necessity, yes. But we also changed in ways we wouldn't have thought possible and now many of us prefer this new way of working. The amount of abandoned office space in cities and corporate parks around the country and the continued use of video meetings makes clear we will never return fully to our old ways. We have reframed what work means and where and when you do it.

It's true that to reimagine what is accepted, we often need to work around significant roadblocks. To help me with the playground project, Rockwell set me up with experts in early childhood and in play as well as a consultant from one of the big playground manufacturers. He was a sweet, older gentleman, but I'm quite certain I drove him mad. He would come into the studio and I would show him ideas.

"We're trying to do this," I'd say. "What about that?"

"That's illegal," he'd respond. "You can't do that. It's not up to code."

He had a manual, a set of rules that make up the safety code for playgrounds. They had given me one, too. This guy would side-eye the binder sitting at my desk, likely noticing it was barely touched. Then he'd grab his dog-eared copy, flagged with notes and tabs and highlights. He always knew exactly which page he wanted.

"Here's what a slide needs to be," he'd say, pointing to page 200 and something. (This manual is a beast.)

"Really?" I'd ask. "A slide can be thirty-five degrees, and this height and this width for children of a certain age? There's no variation? It can only be this?"

"Yes."

The manual was designing the equipment. The rules were designing the play. The real conversation was happening between the manufacturers and the liability insurance companies. Regulations and best practices are important, yes. Safety is important. But to say a slide is this and can only be this is going too far. It is the opposite of design thinking. The tail was wagging the dog except it wasn't even wagging, it was quivering.

Eventually, I tried a different approach.

"What if we don't call it a slide? What if we call it an inclined plane to help children experience adrenaline?"

"Oh," he said.

I had stumped him. From then on, I stopped calling things a slide, a swing, a ladder, or monkey bars. I had to disregard the language because the language was limiting what a playground could be. It was limiting what play could be. I had to name the function of a slide—that it is about experiencing adrenaline—and then find another way to achieve that goal.

RETHINKING THE GOAL

I call this approach name-by-function. You could also call it rethinking the goal. It's one of my favorite exercises, a way to get people to create from their imagination rather than by following instructions. It's the difference between asking kids to "imagine a car" and asking them to "imagine a way to get to school." That instruction—create a way to get to school—is open-ended, suggesting a world of possibilities for getting from point A to point B. Could you walk? Could you fly? Could you climb over rooftops?

What if all sidewalks were moving? What if cities were still designed for horses?

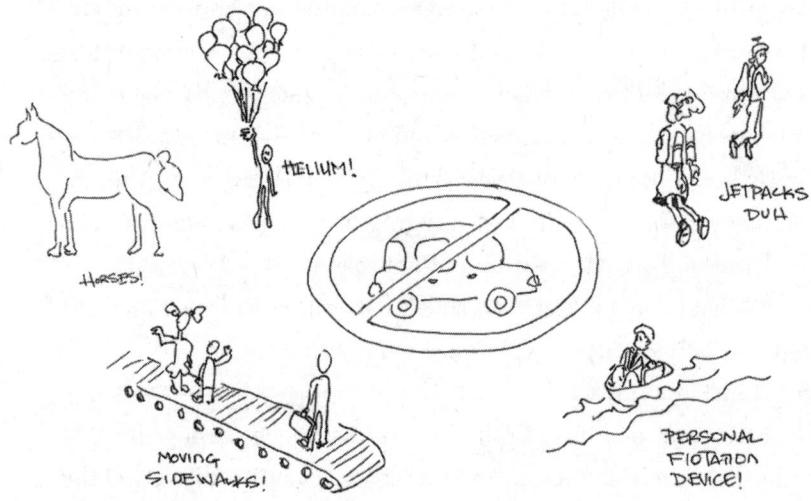

The function (or purpose) here is getting to school and the fun is in exploring the unexpected ways of doing it, creating something (maybe a magic carpet), and then naming that creation (maybe it's yellow and we call it a School Carpet instead of School Bus). Too often, by naming, and defining things by their archetype rather than their function—"car" versus "mode of transportation" or "slide" versus "inclined plane"—we limit the potential outcomes. It's like asking leading questions. There is no space to go in a different direction. Even the most innovative car will still be a car. The way we categorize or name things can limit their potential whereas open-ended language lets us approach the possibilities in a new way. Unpacking the purpose helps get us there.

In Chapter 3, although I didn't name it, I applied the name-by-function exercise when I asked us to consider the purpose of adulthood. We can back up and think about the purpose of play, too. I've done this in some of my workshops. For Nike and the people who work there, play is sports, and competitive sports at that. When I gave a workshop there using Rigamajig, the first goal was to help them experience play more broadly, to embrace the possibilities of free play. As usual, the workshop was also about open-endedness and designing without an end goal in mind. It was about play as a process, not just an outcome or behavior they could design for intentionally.

As we got underway, I was struck by the realization that the team I was working with hadn't ever played together in an open-ended way. They had played sports, and I sensed a great rapport from high-intensity early-morning gym sessions. Yet playing together more loosely, without competitive metrics, creates room for building on ideas and talents that emerge when the unexpected is the goal. It is a beautiful way to get to know other people fully. Is this someone who can take an oddball idea and run with it? Whose imagination can keep up with yours and push you to new places? Will you sit in the grass giggling together, or will you set off on grand adventures? We draw on our early play experiences when we collaborate professionally. In fact, one of my favorite things about collaborating is that while doing so, I can often work out how people played as kids. It is a bit like eating a meal and figuring out how it was made. Who someone is as an adult makes more sense to me once I understand how they played as a child and that's when I know how to work with them.

Working with Rigamajig allowed the group from Nike to connect in this new way and to see play in this way. In these situations, as when I am teaching, I anticipate adult hang-ups with their role within the collaboration and the overwhelming adult need to be good at things. Participants at a place like Nike tend to be highly achieving people who like to succeed. The group included executives and executive assistants, but I didn't know which was which and to their credit, I couldn't tell the difference. When I do this exercise, I structure the prompt so that it requires both "builders" and "storytellers." In other words, someone who isn't comfortable diving in to figure out how to make a structure can stay busy imagining and considering how to tell the story. The exercise happens so quickly that no one thinks to wonder if their work is good or correct.

The Nike designers noticed and acknowledged their own insecurities around free play and making things. Some became aware of being competitive in the absence of competition. They caught themselves looking around to make sure their construction was tallest even though height had nothing to do with the prompt. Others described being excited by the open-endedness of the exercise. In the world of sports, there is a built-in hierarchy in which able-bodied, strong humans tend to excel. Here, with Rigamajig, strength was immaterial. If the goal of play previously had been to be the best, for an afternoon, at least, they felt that the goal—and rewards—of play was to be in it, to pretend and to be present with one another.

We can rethink the goal of everyday tasks, too. What's the intention? The motivation? If you back up and consider the big picture—the goal—of what you're trying to do, there's a chance to be playful in finding other ways to accomplish it. Do we need to design (or buy) an improved eco-friendly compostable to-go coffee cup, or should we just take ten minutes to sit and drink coffee from a mug? Do we need a better way to drink coffee, or do we need a nap? Maybe a shorter workday is the solution. Whatever you think of Marie Kondo and her mania for tidying up, the exercise she created in which you hold your belongings one by one and ask whether they spark joy gets at something important. Don't take anything for granted. Don't assume you need what you think you need. Take your activities out one by one and ask what they're really all about.

A friend of mine was struggling with getting chores done while watching his kids. They wanted to help but he'd find himself redoing their work. He described folding laundry with them as two steps forward and three steps back. I suggested he rethink the goal. Perhaps it could be twofold (no pun intended). What if the goal is partly learning how to fold, but more broadly, spending quality time together? Does it matter if a six-year-old's T-shirt is wrinkled when you pull it out of the drawer? They playtested this with great success. The outcome of the "folding" included some origami T-shirts and elaborately twisted underpants, but the outcome of the quality time was a blast. Folding became something they did playfully together. My friend has since applied this approach to cleaning the children's bedrooms together. The goal isn't that it gets done efficiently; the goal is that things get put away. They play music and the toys dance their way into the bins. Cleanup is part of the play.

When you rethink everyday tasks, you're likely to slow down as a result. Prepare to be surprised. Sometimes the goal is not what you think it is. Say you set out on a hike with young children believing the goal is to get to the top of the mountain trail you're on. Then the kids begin to meander, chasing birds and poking in the dirt. The adults can remind themselves that their purpose was to be outside as a family, or to gather rocks for the growing collection on the kitchen windowsill—the destination was arbitrary. Mission accomplished.

If what you really want is to stay connected with a friend, but time is tight, consider what you could do beyond scheduling an entire evening together. You could call to catch up. You could text a quick joke. You could even go old school and send a postcard. The message: *Hey, I'm thinking of you.*

Rethinking the goal could mean questioning the purpose of meetings or business trips. It might mean shifting how you think about the goal of a home or work project in the first place. I once worked with a team of car designers tasked with "keeping kids occupied in the back seat." Together, we changed the design brief to this: "How can the experience of getting from point A to point B be more playful?"

Speaking of staying occupied in the back seat, are you feeling nostalgic for your childhood play but not sure it serves you today? Consider what that play was giving you. Unpack its purpose. If, like me, you loved to climb trees, maybe it was the change of perspective on the world, the literal height, that appealed. Or maybe it was a way to hide, blending in behind the leaves and branches. If tree-climbing no longer feels achievable (maybe you've got a bum knee or there are no appropriate trees where you live), there's nothing to stop you from finding a rooftop to hang out on or making a point of visiting the observation deck of a skyscraper when you happen to be near one. Once again, embrace the possibilities.

SOMETIMES SIMPLE IS BEST

In reimagining a playground, I asked myself what purpose the various pieces of standard equipment served. Then I sketched children in different positions that represented play or sensory experiences and imagined how to get them there. Just as slides are about adrenaline, swings and trampolines are about weightlessness, movement, and letting go of control. A fort is about quiet, secret time. I could design for all of it.

For a while, I dared to contemplate what "junk" we could use in what we were now calling Imagination Playground. I drew up plans for pulling material from the city's waste stream, just as Lady Allen had once done. But I quickly ran up against another constraint. As I've already pointed out, most adults, and certainly most New Yorkers, are not so keen on a dumpy-looking lot filled with construction debris in their neighborhood, and there is no denying that adventure playgrounds are inherently messy even if they enable wonderful types of play. This playground we were designing had to pass code. It had to survive the elements outdoors. And it couldn't look like garbage.

The challenge was to make the mess palatable. In the end, I didn't create inclined planes or climbing structures or any of the things with which I'd tortured that playground regulations consultant. Instead, my various field trips and conversations gave me a different idea. What about the staple of loose parts play: building blocks? What if we blew those up, made them giant? That would capture some of the play values in adventure playgrounds but in a modular fashion that didn't require much maintenance and was safe enough to require only minimal supervision. I could create a set of outsized foam building blocks in different shapes and sizes. They would come with no instructions. They would just be there, an entire playground of (attractive!) loose parts that children could make into whatever they wanted.

These became the Big Blue Blocks. They were inspired by the tried-and-true classic wooden blocks designed by teacher Caroline Pratt in 1913. City and Country, the school Pratt founded in New York, has giant wooden blocks that riff on the now ubiquitous wooden unit block sets Pratt created. Usually made of maple, the basic block is 5 ½ x 2 ¾ inches and then the rest of the set are multiples or fractions of that size. They make sense: Two of these equal that.

What's great about the basic building block is the way it encompasses possibility. It can be anything: a car, a train, a lion, a whale. You don't always want a lion in your story, but if you have a blank block, you can always have a lion when you do want one. I made my blocks the size of a three-year-old child but light enough that a three-year-old child would be able to move them around, pile them up, knock them down. They are blue because that is the stock color for the material, and conveniently, it doesn't show dirt and wear as much as lighter colors.

There was a stage in the development of the design when we took a step back to ask if the basic unit block was too basic. Could they be more interesting and innovative, more beautiful? We thought we must be able to add something, to improve the design in some way other than scale. But the simplicity of building blocks is what makes them work so well. They are hard to improve on. I realized that the more we designed the blocks, the less the children (users) could design with them. Making something look good in pictures doesn't necessarily make it good for play. If we overdesigned the blocks, then we, the designers, would be doing the fun part rather than leaving an opening for kids to jump in and take over the design where we left off.

What could the basic building blocks of possibility be in your adult life? A flight of stairs? An hour? A window? The ingredients you already have in the fridge? A blank sketchbook? We sometimes think we need expensive toys to play, that we need to buy things—tickets, vehicles, sporting equipment. That is when we need to remember the wonder of the cardboard box or a stick and some mud. There is joy in simplicity, there is joy in simply noticing—in attention play. There is possibility in a beach, in a bookcase, in a bustling skyline (have you ever really looked at it?). No complications. No purchase required.

(RE)EDUCATING OURSELVES

For many of us, the resistance we have to the wonders of embracing possibilities lingers from the Western-style education we received as kids. In general, our classrooms look today as they have for a very long time, with rows of desks and the teacher standing at the front of the room imparting knowledge. Too often, the emphasis in our modern style of education is on reproducing that knowledge, not constructing it. In a constructivist model of education, students have space and time to figure it out, explore, do it wrong. Figuratively and literally, they are constructing knowledge. It's hard to be constructivist when you need a right answer. Needing a right answer isn't playful. Extrinsic motivators like grades, bell curves, and rankings become our reason to learn, rather than intrinsic ones like curiosity, interest, and joy. Extrinsic motivation sticks with many of us well into adulthood and makes it very difficult to play in open-ended ways. Because we've been formed by a focus on outcomes, it makes sense that we are lost without defined goals. We've been programmed to think that dillydallying or puttering around is a waste. But the opposite is true: Slowing down and living in the moment without a particular goal is a great way to let yourself find what you want to do, what you're drawn to do, outside of pressure to be productive or efficient in completing a task. Let yourself spend hours putzing in the yard. Moving dirt around feels great. Rearranging the junk drawer brings the satisfaction of sorting and restoring order. Maybe finding some old markers in the back of that drawer is an excuse to do some drawing, or what if you put that stray box of birthday candles to use and celebrated . . . because there's a full moon on a Tuesday? Putzing and puttering is a way to occupy the surface of the mind while leaving space for deeper currents to flow underneath. It can be a way to generate fresh ideas, to lead yourself down an unexpected path.

That path will look slightly different for each of us. We standardize education but humans are not standardizable. Certainly, school didn't reward the things I was good at. I was good at exploring, at creating, at thinking outside the box. I was less good at sitting still, plodding through worksheets, and rote memorization. I was also not so good at playing by rules that I found arbitrary. Apologies to most of my teachers. My friends and I started an underground newspaper in high school as a way of digging into the issues we cared about—such as animal rights and reproductive rights. We were going against the grain in our conservative, rural community. I think most people would agree that writing and distributing your own publication is a good example of self-directed learning and the pursuit of knowledge. But the principal had vowed to expel the culprits once he discovered who they were, and in the end, we got kicked out. It was a bit of a shock to him to find out that we were a high-achieving bunch—the senior class valedictorian, the junior class president, and me, the star of the volleyball team. Eventually, our expulsion was downgraded to a week's suspension. Yet it seemed to me then—and seems to me still—like the wrong message to send to smart students. I'm not alone in feeling that school as I experienced it in a typical American public high school was not designed for me.

In one of the most famous TED Talks of all time (78 million views and counting), British author Sir Ken Robinson asked if schools kill creativity. His answer was straightforward: yes. Creativity is as important as literacy, he argued. And all kids are creative until we squash it out of them. "If you run an education system based on standardization and conformity that suppresses individuality, imagination, and creativity, don't be surprised if that's what it does," Robinson wrote in his book *Creative Schools*. His TED Talk was a plea for the value of making mistakes and being wrong. Adults, he said, have made children afraid of mistakes. "We run our companies this way," he said. "We run education this way." We have created a world where "mistakes are the worst thing you can make." We have designed the playground of our lives with liability top of mind. Robinson believes play is a foundation of creativity and it is a critical part of his call to restructure schooling. "Human flourishing is not a mechanical process," he has argued. "It's an organic process. All you can do is, like a farmer, create the conditions under which [children] will begin to flourish."

I couldn't agree with him more. When I teach college students, I see the other end of childhood and the impact a standardized education system has on young adults, as they enter the next phase of their lives. The instinct to play is already being drummed out of them. The effects of the K–12 education system that most students come through are obvious. After a dozen years in the test-assessment model of education, young people arrive in college overly attached to grades, extrinsic motivation, and validation. They are very risk averse. And these are art students, supposedly the most creative of the bunch in their respective high schools. They learned how to be good at a school, but not necessarily how to learn and be curious. They certainly didn't love learning.

My students were often freaked out by my refusal to tell them what they needed to do to get an A. When I was a student at UC Santa Cruz, there were no grades. At Cranbrook, there were no grades. As a professor, I found grades an unhelpful way of assessing artistic effort and I refused to use them as extrinsic motivators. One semester, I let my students grade themselves. They were harsher than I would have been. I wasn't alone in trying to change things up. Other faculty at RISD went to great extremes to wean students off their obsession with grades. One said to his students, "Everyone is getting an A. Now what do you actually want to make?" He was helping them rethink the goal.

But early on, I saw the limits of what I could do within the system. A student came to me in tears, uncertain about her grade. She was upset that I wasn't giving out progress updates and grades after each exercise. (In part, that was because I didn't know how.) "But you're getting an A!" I said to her. "What's the problem?" She told me she was on a scholarship and that keeping it depended on getting A's. If she wasn't sure how to do that, she didn't know how to prepare or work. We were both stuck.

Because middle and high school education is too structured, college students are uncomfortable with uncertainty. Because childhood lacks opportunities for free play, young adults aren't fluent in creating their own structure. Because children aren't in the habit of keeping themselves occupied, young adults feel helpless without guidance. Because children consume rather than create their own play or activities or interests, they are uncomfortable with open-ended activities. Pardon my broad statements. I'm glad there are exceptions to this, but I wish there were more.

Too many youth activities are structured competitively and end up teaching young people to stick with something for improvement or mastery rather than enjoyment. It's a message that only gets stronger as we get older. I hear all the time from adults who say they loved soccer but weren't good at it, so they quit. Or they loved ballet but got too tall and couldn't become a professional dancer, so they gave it up. Too often, we think the only point in pursuing something is to excel at it or get a job doing it. What if the point is in the doing? I try to value the joy I get from things, even when I'm terrible at them.

On my first day in the classroom as a professor, however, I wasn't thinking such big thoughts. I was terrified. I had been hired to teach industrial design to undergraduates at Syracuse University, but I had never taken an undergraduate design class myself. Now I had to teach one. The chair of my new department threw me in at the deep end. He assigned me to teach three classes including an introduction to design course. When I asked for a syllabus for the introductory class, he said there wasn't one. Talk about open-ended. Not only did I not know what the students needed to learn, I knew nothing about the nuts and bolts of teaching—how to pace a class or a semester, how much time to allow for projects, how much reading to assign. And no one was going to tell me any of that. I had to figure it out. That meant considering all the possible ways of doing it.

I asked myself what the students needed to think about, and decided we would start with product systems and cycles. For example, with a toothbrush, designers think about not just the brush, but the paste, holder, floss, and mouthwash—the whole ritual of oral hygiene. That is a product system. A product cycle concerns what something is made of, how it's made, who's making it, and where it goes when it's no longer needed. As we walked through examples and visited a Waste Management (recycling) facility, I often found myself at the chalkboard facilitating conversations and drawing diagrams to visualize the interconnectedness of it all. Then we moved on to honing skills like sketching, modeling, and using software to support their visions. I always recommend designing with pen, paper, and prototypes before moving into digital tools that tend to make the process less playful by telling you what you can and can't do.

In trying to help my students learn about design, it became clear to me what they needed: a radical shift in perspective. These were students who entered school wanting to design shoes and cars. Or maybe phone cases. They wanted to design products, but they had limited imagination about what those could be outside of resurfacing existing products and models of use—adding cool colors at the end or tweaking a product just enough to entice consumers into feeling they needed the latest version. ("Skinning" is the industrial design term for changing the way something looks to make it seem new.) It's a version of the common roadblock to innovation among adults who've been working in the same company or organization for years. Presented with a different approach, they say, "But this is the way we've always done it."

Rigidity of thinking showed up in how students thought about art itself and what qualified as art. Many kids, coming out of high school, are lucky to have had a painting and drawing class, maybe ceramics. That's all they know of art. When I served on admissions committees reviewing portfolios, that's all we would see—painting, drawing, and ceramic sculpture. Yet later I would find out that some of my students had spent their time outside of school building robots or a tree house or helping their mother construct a patio. It hadn't occurred to them to put those things in the portfolio they used to apply to art school, because they didn't think of such things as art. If an admissions committee is looking at a handful of (usually not great) paintings, but in the meantime, you are building robots, tell us about the robots!

In adults, rigidity of thinking often shows up in how we use our time, in where we think we can play, in what jobs we think we want. The uncertainty of embracing alternate possibilities can be foundation shaking. It can mean stepping into the unknown.

And hey, we have had our hearts broken, we've been disappointed, we have lost people and jobs and we hold tight to what we know because it is comfortable and feels safe. We have even more reasons than young people do to fear change.

I needed to break my students' thinking. My goal became nothing less than dismantling everything they had just learned in high school. Okay, I don't really mean everything; I mean their understanding of why they were learning, their relationship to their work and what it meant to be engaged and smart and talented. I wanted to usurp the associations students arrive with so they could make art without fear of being bad at it. Students—and all of us—need to practice doing things in ways that are unrelated to winning or excelling. I try to suspend the need to be great. I rarely show examples of what I'm after because I don't want students to get too attached to one idea of success. I insist that students show their process while they work. When they say, "It's not done" *and* "It's not right" *and* "It's not perfect," that makes them want to keep it hidden.

That's when I first got the idea for name-by-function. I asked my students, What problems do you see? What would you design? This unpacking of purpose stimulated conversation and sparked ideas. It loosened up my students' thought processes. It got them beyond skinning shoes and cars. I knew right away that it was an exercise I would conduct with all my classes. Each time I did it, I appreciated its power. We were starting at the very beginning, asking, Why? Name-by-function doesn't assume you are going to make a new version of what's been made before. It assumes you don't know what you are making. It questions everything. By definition it embraces *all* the possibilities.

Just as I suggest you do, I use play to invite students to be brave, bold, and unattached to success. In an assignment called Body-ation, students take a picture of themselves in a pose and then design ways to get into that posture. The process recalls how I worked to innovate playgrounds, drawing young children in different positions, and working out how to get them there. One student photographed herself in a side plank position and designed from there. She sketched a bicycle that was ridden sideways, a space-saving bed closet, a tube-slide transportation system for cities, and at least seven other concepts, each more absurd than the previous. Her work was a glorious celebration of fun and adventure. Body-ation reconnects students with the fact that they do know how to play.

Another favorite assignment I use is called A Series of Movements to Make a Form. Students set up an experience for their classmates in which each person's movement contributes to a form. In one of these experiences, a student created a die with various instructions printed on each side (pinch, kick, knead, etc.). As classmates rolled the die, they had to manipulate a piece of clay according to the instructions. Another student spread sand on the floor and distributed instructions to jump, slide, or skip, thereby creating an original pattern in the sand. There is a give-and-take in such an exercise. I love watching them play with it and talking to them as they do it. The form of the clay or the sand always changes a little bit as we go. I wouldn't call it codesign. It's much more like playing. I create the conditions—minimal constraints, lack of judgment, a focus on exploration as the goal—and they create the materials that invite their peers to play.

There is enormous potential for doing this in our work lives. The rules or constraints can be arbitrary. My assigned goal for my students was using movement to create a 3-D form. Yours might be to use materials from your recycling bin to express the ideas from a brainstorming meeting. Does rolling the die make it easier to choose an idea to follow? If you've committed to giving that chosen idea twenty minutes, it will be easier for your team to go all-in discussing it even if the idea doesn't initially appeal. If you lead a team, the important element is creating conditions where people feel safe sharing the seed of an idea, knowing that it will be explored collectively with enthusiasm. Success in this process is exploration not efficiency. The outcome is a new approach, not necessarily a viable solution.

Part of the conversation we need in education is about being a consumer of your education versus being an active participant. In the same vein, we can ask what it means to be an active rather than passive participant in your adult life. What's the difference? Engaging. Asking questions. Shaping your own experience. Embracing the possibilities of learning. As the wise artist and educator Corita Kent, also known as Sister Mary Corita, put it, the duties of a student are to "pull everything out of your teacher. Pull everything out of your fellow students." For the record, she also said that the general duties of a teacher are to "pull everything out of your students." Those ideas are part of Kent's well-known "10 Rules," which I have turned to again and again in my teaching. They are simple but radical. And they can inspire anyone inside and outside of the classroom.

Everything is an experiment, Kent says. And there are no mistakes. "There is no win and no fail. There is only make." Kent urges trust, self-discipline, doing the work, and trying to be happy. "Enjoy yourself. It's lighter than you think." And finally, she urges breaking the rules, including her own. It's a set of guidelines I share with students any way I can. I post them on classroom walls, hand them out as documents, and show students a documentary about Kent and her rules. The short film was made in the 1960s and has a slow pace and cinematic pauses typical of the time. My students initially squirm and look bored at having to listen to a nun talk about ways of looking. But after five minutes or so, they settle in and seem to appreciate her wisdom.

One piece of that wisdom is something we can all adopt anywhere, any time: Kent's "frames for looking." Kent used a small piece of paper with holes cut out of the middle, but you can also just use your fingers. Hold the ad hoc frame up to the world—to the opposite side of the street, to a corner of your office, to the view out the window. It adds edges, it changes proportions and perspective, it highlights details you might have otherwise missed. "Sometimes you can take the whole of the world in and sometimes you need a small piece to take in," Kent said. She assigned her own art students two hours of walking the streets just looking around them. I often see my students using Sister Mary Corita's "frames for looking" in their work.

POSSIBILITIES AND CONSTRAINTS

These miniature frames are a form of constraint—a way of literally limiting what we can see so that, figuratively, we can see more. Earlier, I described some of the constraints I include in my assignment about accessing play for adults. Sometimes the possibilities for play or anything else feel so broad as to be overwhelming. What Kent does so well is spell out the necessary balance between open-endedness and constraints. We all—children, college students, adults—need that balance. At their most useful, constraints provide structure, which is not antithetical to a lack of instructions or predetermined goals. Constraints are sets of conditions to work within. They relate to materials—tools for creating—or to the amount of time spent, not concepts. I might say students can use one piece of paper, some tape, and one hour of time to make something that expresses a mood. Open-ended conceptually, constraints are the How and the students imagine the What. They give creativity some boundaries—something to push against. They are not rules that define what something can be or should be.

We use constraints in multiple ways, even though we might not realize it. Consider a writer who uses free-writing spurts in a notebook to overcome the terror of the blank page. The constraints: the time limit, the notebook, and the lack of judgment about what to write or whether it is any good. Or in rock climbing, there's a rule to keep climbers from getting stuck: Just move. If you can't see how to go up, go sideways, or even down again. Just move.

I once saw a piece of performance art in which fifteen dancers essentially played freely onstage. A few days after the show, I spoke with the choreographer, Anna, who shared with me how difficult the process of creating it had been. Her goal was to avoid hierarchy and create a collaborative, open-ended project that would explore how dance could be informed by free play and still take the shape of a performance for an audience. She had started rehearsals by inviting everyone to contribute and collectively make the performance what they wanted. That turned out to be too big, too open. The participants were willing, but they didn't seem to know where to start. They needed a squiggle on the page, so to speak, something to react to, to push against. Anna provided some prompts and those ultimately led to the piece I saw.

Close your eyes and become a creature.

Giant rock feet.

Tell me what to do. (One dancer would say this out loud and another dancer would respond.)

Ask the group for help with something that you can't do on your own.

That last one led to people being carried around like Superman as if they were flying, being pulled by their feet, pinned to the wall, and held like a baby.

The limits created freedom for the dancers—they could play within those parameters, knowing they were on the same page as their collaborators. The minimal structure along with established time frames and trust in one another created the conditions for them to free play within their chosen medium: movement.

Halloween costumes are another place where constraints can be just what's needed. I love imagining and creating costumes more than almost anything. If I could, I would go out in the street and offer to make costumes for other people's children. But not everyone sees Halloween as an unadulterated opportunity to be creative. For some people, the planning ahead, the hours of sewing or gluing, the pressure to be creative piles up into a headache. What if they declare some constraints? Four hours to make a costume. Only use things we already have in the house. Do it together (for parent and child, friends, or a couple).

We can benefit from constraints in our work lives, too. For example, turning off Wi-Fi access, putting your phone across the room, forcing yourself to talk about an idea in different contexts or even different vocabulary. Through much of my process, I remind myself, *You have everything you need.* That helps me avoid the impulse to look for ideas and answers (and distractions) online. A book of advice for writers struggling to turn an idea into a fully fleshed out book offers the following exercise, which can apply in other contexts. The advice is to take the idea—the topic used as an example is ocean rowing—and write twelve separate three-sentence paragraphs describing twelve very different books on ocean rowing. It could be a how-to. It could be a travel memoir. It could be a meditation on sea and sky and physical effort. And so on. The constraint is fitting the same idea into different jackets, so to speak. As a result, the would-be writer gets a sense of what feels like the best fit. That kind of exercise can work in any number of professions—perhaps in rethinking uses of a product or coming up with out-of-the-box marketing ideas. It's a constraint that forces some sideways thinking and might generate newfound clarity.

Similarly, some cultural traditions can be made more playful if we let go of our need to perform *adult*. Potluck dinners loosen up the entertainment playbook and allow for gatherings that might feel like too much work for one person to pull off alone. The constraint is that everyone participates and so what if we end up with several versions of potatoes? Holiday decorating is a source of joy for some and an enormous obligation for others (and perhaps a bit of both for many). Congratulations to those who have a vision and bring it to life every year on their own. If that's play for you, then go for it. But there can be play in relaxing the "rules" of decorating. Homemade ornaments don't take themselves too seriously and kids love to see their own creations. There is beauty in the process and in a Christmas tree decorated with love and family spirit.

A constraint can also be thought of as a prompt, a suggestion that pushes you toward play. Sometimes prompts are environmental. Some spaces and events naturally facilitate free play by creating the conditions for free play to arise. The Burning Man festival is a space created expressly for embracing curiosity, for releasing judgment, and for engaging in open-ended play. Music festivals can be the same way. They facilitate socializing, dancing, singing along, and being in the moment. Public parks that are open for a variety of uses let us play softball, play catch, lie on our backs gazing up at the treetops, or play with our dogs. The pandemic prompted us to more thoroughly explore the outdoors immediately around us, whether that was a corner of a city park, a suburban cul-de-sac, or the woods, and we saw we could use those places in new ways. There is no reason we can't keep using those spaces in those new ways. Pride parades and parties are as judgment-free as they come. Seedy bars are another place where we can let it all hang out; we don't have to worry about how we're dressed, whether we spilled ketchup, or whether we're laughing too loud. Think about the places you feel most free and take yourself there more often. Or you can try to re-create those circumstances in other parts of your life.

You may wonder how to differentiate between constraints that limit creativity and those that inspire. If I give too many constraints, they become distracting and the project, overly complicated. If I don't give any, my students feel overwhelmed and don't know where to start. I give assignments with a bunch of constraints. But I tell students to ignore any constraints that aren't useful. The same principles apply to adults finding ways to give themselves permission not to be brilliant but to play with ideas and curiosity. Give yourself constraints to start and then ignore the ones that don't feel helpful. In creativity, it helps to feel supported, even if you are just supporting yourself.

If my department chair at Syracuse had given me a syllabus to follow, I most certainly would have ignored a lot of it. I wanted it as a starting place because I didn't have any references. I wanted to know the rules so I could work out if I wanted to break them. At RISD, my next employer, I had the opposite problem (ironic, since I had more experience). There was a syllabus for the intro class I taught, and I was meant to follow it to the letter. With 150 students taking the class from six different professors, the concern was that everyone needed to cover the same material. Or so the department chair thought. The next chair changed it up and told us professors to do it our own way—a reminder that judgments about the right and wrong of any way of doing something are in the eye of the beholder. Maybe you've had the same experience with a new boss, who changes things up in ways that might not have seemed possible. Our knee-jerk reaction is often to resist the new approach—change is hard. But if we leave ourselves open to the possibilities, we might be surprised by the results.

I often wonder what beholders would make of my classroom and how surprised they would be by what we get up to. My students and I spend a lot of time talking about curiosity and what it means to be an artist beyond external validation. We talk about finding other motivation: Can being a good artist be enough? What is a good artist? Is that motivating you to make good art? What about curiosity? Why do I have to give you extrinsic rewards? Why do you have to gamify your life to feel motivated? Students are okay with this for a bit and then within a couple days, there is panic written all over their faces again. But we persist. We reframe how to exist in the world. We adopt new ways of looking. My students' first step toward letting themselves be artists is to let themselves play.

Some days were wonderful, and I knew I had succeeded. I would look around the room during an exercise called bodystorming, in which students use their bodies to develop ideas. Somebody was doing a headstand. Someone else was rolling around on the floor. And a group of students had configured their bodies into a roller coaster to explain an engineering principle. In that moment I stopped everyone in their tracks and asked them to look around. Is this rigorous? What are we doing? How are we going to justify this use of precious studio time? How will you talk about this in your portfolio? Beautiful conversations would come out of that. To my great satisfaction, my students would defend this seemingly disorderly conduct as the process. This is as rigorous as 3-D modeling exercises, they would argue. We were discovering what we value and why. And we were playing while doing it.

Our new thinking, moving beyond cars and shoes, led us to new ideas about what learning could be, and what "counted" as productive. Even though my students didn't always know what would come of our creative processes, they willingly jumped in. They found themselves in places—physically and conceptually—that they wouldn't have imagined before. They fully embraced the possibilities.

To embrace possibility as adults, we'll need to do the same. To venture out of our safety zones and trust that we'll wind up somewhere new and unexpected. The process of doing that can be reason enough, but you may go somewhere wonderful. There is joy in imagining outside of what we know and what is familiar. You can play your way to somewhere new.

6

RELEASE JUDGMENT

My friend Garrett was once at a work retreat in Wyoming. After a day of meetings, he and his boss found themselves waiting for a shuttle back to their hotel. They were standing at the end of a long driveway by a metal fence that marked the boundary of a horse ranch, and they didn't know how long their wait would be. They might wait two minutes or twenty.

Garrett climbed up and stood on the lowest rung of the fence with his arms slung over the top and leaned forward to watch the horses. Next to him, his boss climbed a rung higher and perched there, with only his waist supported by the top railing. *Huh,* thought Garrett, *what's he up to?* He decided to test the play waters. He slowly pulled himself up to stand on the top bar, balancing precariously with his arms outflung. Accepting the challenge, his boss did the same—with some struggle, he stood up, extended his arms, and turned sideways. Like young gymnasts just learning to walk on a balance beam, they started moving along the fence line. There were a few slips and wobbles but by the time the shuttle came, their agility had improved and their game had escalated to running along the top bar, chasing each other, and treating each post as a new kind of challenge. Hop over this one. Step sideways over that one. Spin around on the third one.

These were professional colleagues, and they were playing. They had chosen not to worry about using the time productively by, say, catching up on the emails they'd missed during the day. They had mutually decided the fun to be had was worth far more than whatever work might get done. And they had quickly gotten over any worry about whether this was appropriate behavior for two grown men.

I suspect most of you have not done anything like that since you were young, especially not with your boss. Worries about how we will be perceived when we play hold us back. You don't have to be a self-described weirdo like me to feel judged. We all feel the gaze of others on our appearance, our behavior, our choices, our work. We judge ourselves, too. We worry about what we said or what we didn't say, about whether people like us or dislike us, about getting things right and getting things wrong, about not being good at something. So much judgment! No wonder we play so rarely as adults. Friends tell me they feel judged when being publicly playful. It makes it harder to go there. We bump up against social norms that tell us play is for children. We buy into the idea that adulthood is about productivity, or that there are appropriate and inappropriate ways to play for our gender and our age. We don't want to stand out or look silly, we don't want to waste time, or we don't see the point. Not here. Not now. Not you. Not like that.

Even I sometimes feel that way. When I'm chatty in line at the grocery store, I worry that others will think I'm making the whole process take longer. That I'm getting in the way of the collective need to be efficient. Or when I'm being silly, I worry about being thought an unserious person. So much of adulthood is about trying to communicate that we should be taken seriously that we seem to believe that the only way to do that is to be serious, all the time.

But play can be—should be—a judgment-free zone. It's an opportunity to try new things or do things we love no matter how adept at them we are or whether they are serious or not. Being unserious is the point! When the joy is in the doing not the outcome, play becomes a welcome place of relaxation and release, of exploration and enthusiasm. This is why the second element in my formula for free play for adults is releasing judgment, letting go of the worries and expectations we carry for ourselves and others. After all, it's hard to embrace possibilities without then also releasing judgment. When Shaka did yoga at the airport, they embraced and then released, deciding not to worry about what other people might think. When Garrett first climbed that fence, then kept climbing up and up in a physical call-and-response with his boss, he embraced, then released. Releasing judgment allows us to be our true selves or to explore being someone else for a bit and to see others as their true selves or in a new light. It allows us to do things we might normally shy away from, to shake loose our preconceived notions. It allows for mindfulness and presence rather than preoccupation. It lets us willingly receive whatever happens. We ease up, we are amenable and unbiased.

NO RIGHT OR WRONG WAY

This vision of play as judgment-free is not a fantasy. It happens when we let it. I hear the stories all the time. Two old friends on a weeklong road trip spent hours every day singing at the top of their lungs to '70s and '80s rock anthems even though neither of them knew any of the lyrics. One day in a rather stuffy office, a manager put out art supplies before a meeting and then watched with pleasure as, one by one, her colleagues picked up markers and started coloring. The woman who told me the story was one of those colleagues. She surprised herself by how much she enjoyed it. Art wasn't something she felt she was good at or gravitated toward as an adult, yet she tapped into her own playfulness and even a little glee while noodling around with color and line.

Friends of The High Line is a nonprofit organization that worked with the New York City Department of Parks & Recreation to transform a historic, elevated freight rail line on the lower West Side of Manhattan into an unusual public park, which now runs for about twenty blocks above the streets and sometimes through buildings. The group wanted to include an element that would appeal to parents and children—something visitors could play with, in other words, for ten minutes or two hours. "I wish we could just give them a bunch of two-by-fours," said the then-head of public programs. I decided to figure out a way to do just that. A mess of building materials seemed quite natural to encounter in such a place, where you see the detritus of industry, the scars of the machines that used to roam there. It would sing the siren song of exploration that rings out from any pile of junk. The things in those piles are already unfinished or broken, so you can't go wrong. Experiment, expand your play.

As with the Big Blue Blocks, I proposed a set of loose parts that could be pulled out for play. But these were made of wood and could be put away in a storage container that looked like an art crate. Initially, we called it the High Line Children's Work-yard Kit (a nod to Nancy Rudolph, a photographer who coined the term "workyard" while documenting "junk playgrounds" in NYC and Europe). I later renamed it Rigamajig. It really is a glorified pile of construction debris, a set of large wood pieces that attach to each other every which way as a building system. The materials—wood, bolts, rope—feel special to kids, like we are trusting them with real materials. And while those materials pro-vide constraints, the outcomes they make possible are open-ended. It isn't just about embracing possibilities. The lack of instructions encourages a lack of judgment that is freeing. There's no right or wrong way of playing with Rigamajig and everyone senses that. I also knew instinctively that the system couldn't rely on tools. Losing a critical tool while trying to make something yanks you out of the flow of play. My design goal was playful creation, not learning the importance of being organized. (That isn't to say that tools can't be fun! As my stepfather's garage assistant, my entire job was wrench retrieval and delivery, and I came up with ump-teen elaborate ways to do it. I'd commandeer the rolling sled thing and pretend to swim under the chassis, belly down, doing the frog in nonlinear paths. Or I'd flip to my back and do the backstroke around to bring him whichever wrench he needed.)

After years of watching people of all ages encountering Rigamajig, I've noticed a clear pattern. First, they explore the pieces and get familiar with the system: "Oh, I see. The pieces connect like this," they say. And "I get it, two of these are as long as one of those." They inevitably start to build something randomly and then comes a moment when they create with intention. Maybe they connect a few pieces, and a cart begins to emerge. That inspires them to go further and make it a dune buggy. But then the creation will morph and shift. "That looks like a head. It's a flying sea monster!" At some point the pretend play begins, where they imagine a story, playing in or on the thing they've made. Now they're riding the sea monster through crashing waves, until eventually they need a boat. So, they set about building a boat, back to the creating, figuring out how to use what they have to support the story they're telling. It's a loose and circular kind of play. And it's a useful framework for entering into play without planning or expectation: explore, build randomly, create intentionally, tell a story, explore again.

When we playtested the early version of Rigamajig, I observed a brother and sister, five and six years old, who spent an hour working together intently. The resulting creation was wonderfully odd, with four legs, a long body, and two curving planks jutting down to the floor in front as well as a short limb sticking out on the left. As time wound down, I asked the siblings to tell me about it.

"Oh, it's a spaceship waterslide," the boy told me.

He eagerly pointed out which part was the waterslide and which part was the spaceship's landing gear. Then he launched into impressive detail about where to enter and where the captain sat.

I noticed a puzzled look on his sister's face, and I wondered why she wasn't joining in. Finally, she piped up. "That's not what it is!" she announced. "Those are wings! This is a fairy elephant. It flies when you ask it and uses magic to do stuff." She elaborated about the magic, which led to a debate about whether the slope of the planks was for water or elephant things.

I listened, baffled not by their divergent descriptions but by what it meant for the hour I had watched them play together. It was the first time I'd seen that happen, where two children had totally different interpretations. And although they disagreed, they didn't really care. It wasn't strange to them. While they were building, they were collaborating, discussing which piece should go where. They were on the same page. You take this and

I'll hold that. Let's move that over there. How can we get this to stay up? They did all that without ever needing to decide or agree on what they were making. They were free to have it be whatever they each envisioned. There was no right way.

That is just what I was after. Rigamajig is an invitation to collective imagining. Because there is no one way to engage with it, no one is an expert—even when children and adults play together. There is no hierarchy of who is good and who is bad at it. If anything, the younger players are at an advantage because they tend to be more comfortable working with the unfamiliar, even if one person is working toward a spaceship and the other toward a fairy elephant.

That said, I've since seen adults do something very similar. I once hosted a workshop in Italy with fifty or so participants from all over Europe. There were some language barriers, but nonetheless, while they were building, everything proceeded beautifully. As we moved into the wrap-up phase, I prompted the groups to tell a story about what they had made. That's when it became clear that these adults were just like that brother and sister. A group that included people speaking four different languages had settled on Italian to communicate within the group and English to explain their work to the rest of us. Standing around an elaborate Rigamajig contraption, the first person began. "It floats and these are satellites for moving between clouds." The group burst into laughter, and someone blurted out, "It does?! I thought those were ladders from the ground!" At which point another member of the group interjected: "What? That is a vertical garden hanging from a hot-air balloon!" No one cared. If anything, it added to the fun.

This is what can happen in a state of play and a state of acceptance, where judgment is left at the door. I was gratified to see it, because it can be harder for adults to achieve that level of equanimity than it is for children. They are more likely to say, "How am I supposed to know where that plank goes if I don't know what we're building?" Those multilingual adults in Italy exemplified the joys of letting go of that need to know. And they were a reminder that sometimes communication isn't about understanding each other perfectly, it is about learning how others see differently and accepting those differences.

PLAYTEST LIFE

When those two inventive children were telling me about their creation, I was keenly attuned to their experience and not my own ideas about what they should be doing because, as I said, we were playtesting. Remember that is the phase in design where we give a prototype to people and see what happens when they play with it. Sometimes kids engage with a toy just as we expected. Sometimes they don't. We don't expect the prototypes to be perfect; in fact, often I'll playtest something that's incomplete so I can learn from what doesn't work.

Adults can learn from playtesting, too. In that context, it means being committed to curiously trying. Trying without judgment and without being invested in outcome. Being invested in not being invested. Playtesting is a playful way to frame moments in everyday life as experiments or explorations, then notice what works, what appeals to you, and what doesn't. At my home in rural Rhode Island, affectionately dubbed Camp Fun, we playtested ways to cook in the fireplace when rain kept us from the bonfire. We playtested the karaoke machine at the pool. The ethos was that everyone tried things with enthusiasm and curiosity. Success meant having fun together, so it didn't require much more than our willingness to roll with it. When you playtest something, no single person is responsible for it "working" and everyone participates in evaluating it. Playtesting includes reflection and the assumption that everything is malleable. We change as we go.

A friend of mine and her husband once drove most of the way across the country in an electric vehicle. They were new to the charging game, and they knew it would get challenging out there in the long stretches of highway that cross the middle of the United States. Their solution was to declare that they were playtesting the whole experience. They made their best plan for how to tackle the trip and keep the car sufficiently charged—locating hotels with chargers, keeping books handy for the long waits to recharge, limiting exploration far from the main road—but they acknowledged ahead of time that it might not always go as planned and they would see what worked. That approach made it easier to be patient when charging machines didn't work or when they found out the advertised range on their car was wildly optimistic. It made it easier to laugh in the face of adversity. They joined forces in evaluating as they went and changed their strategy accordingly—and had a lot of fun—along the way.

At the office, you could playtest having meetings outside or sitting on the floor. That's a way of saying we think we could use a change, and we don't know if this is going to work, but let's just try it. At a conference, someone told me about going outside for a meeting with her team. Being outside in the sun perked everyone up, but sitting in the grass was uncomfortable. So the next time, they found some picnic tables.

You can playtest a route to work or a recipe for dinner or a new arrangement of furniture in the living room. Maybe your family regularly holds a game night, and you play rummy all the time. You might make up a new rule and playtest it. Whether or not the rule gets adopted will be up to the group once you see how it goes. A few games—like the Metagame, a card game for adults—require you to make up and change the rules. Or consider a night out for a group of friends. Not everyone wants the pressure of choosing the restaurant or the movie. What if the others don't like it? What matters more: the quality of the food, the vibe, or the price? Different members of the group can reasonably be expected to have different priorities. But if a group of friends can agree ahead of time on the goal, they can playtest their choices. Are they going out because they want to try a hip new restaurant? Or are they getting together because they're overdue for a good catch-up? More than once I've found myself with a large group after an art opening or event and we have no reservations or plan. I try to get everyone on the same page. "Listen, we can wander around for thirty minutes, stand outside for another hour, then maybe get a table at a place we know, or we can just go somewhere with bad lighting and dumb food, but we'll be eating in twenty minutes. If the goal is to keep hanging out, let's shift our standards here."

Sex is perhaps the ultimate opportunity for playtesting. There are lots of different ways to do it and some require one person to prompt or suggest. Sex in the spirit of playtesting would say, we're both going to give it our all with curiosity and a lack of judgment and then we're both going to evaluate whether it was satisfying, whether it was any fun. In playtesting, no one is selling or convincing, rather offering "What if we . . ."

How do you know what you like or what your lover likes if you haven't tried it? Playtesting brings out our curiosity and communication, so it's a great fit for connecting. Both partners are paying attention to each other and noticing the dynamic formed in the play. As psychotherapist Esther Perel says, "a conversation about fantasy is about play, curiosity, transcending the limits of reality and moving beyond your usual boundaries."

Early in one relationship, my partner and I agreed to playtest something new that neither of us had experienced. By framing it as playtesting, neither of us was hurt when midway through we started laughing and said "Is this working? Should we change something and keep trying or learn from this epic fail and move on?" They were more invested than I was in the idea, so we changed it up a few times, checking in along the way. Without the playtesting lens, we couldn't have done that, and it would have been written off as "not our thing." Instead, we wound up with an entirely new way of playing and I got a new perspective to understand someone I love.

If you're looking for ways to emphasize free play over competitive play, you can playtest ways to flip the assumed advantage in certain activities. What's a game that short people are better at? (Maybe a variation on limbo?) How can you hack the rules to shift the advantage to the less vertically gifted? Or what's a game that people who aren't coordinated can play well? (Cards or charades, perhaps?) When I play Operation with my six-year-old friend Artie, I play with my left hand even though I'm right-handed.

This makes it harder for me, and a more equitable game for us both since I have forty-three years' advantage honing my fine-motor skills. My goal isn't to win, but to have fun with my friend. There are ways to adjust games that require a lot of skill and loosen things up. Take scramble golf. Everyone takes a turn and then each team plays their better ball, no matter who hit it. And there are plenty of activities where the barrier to entry is low, and the group benefits from many levels of mastery. That's part of the great appeal of karaoke—the best performers are the ones who are all-in, whether or not they are on-tune.

QUESTION NORMALCY

For children, playtesting is unnecessary. They play because playing is instinctive and socially the norm in childhood. It's what we expect of kids and what we want them to do. For adults, as we have established, not so much. Many forms of adult play teeter on the edge of violating the informal rules that govern behavior in society. Sometimes, adult play tips right over that edge. Here's where external judgment really rears its head. The external rules become internalized, and we usually police ourselves as much as each other. Norms can be a positive force when they involve treating people well, or thinking about the greater good, but there are also norms that demonize harmless behavior.

Nearly everyone who takes an Intro to Social Psychology class in college is asked to do an assignment in which they intentionally go out and violate a social norm and then analyze the experience. One such assignment offers up a list of suggested violations such as singing loudly on a public bus, subway, or train, jumping up and down while waiting in a checkout line, or getting into an elevator with strangers and introducing yourself.

After they violate the norm, students are asked, "Was it uncomfortable, fun, liberating, scary, or something else?"

What's interesting to me about this assignment is that it's a list of ways you could play in public. While it acknowledges that some of that behavior might be "fun," it essentially assumes that "normal" behavior isn't playful. The instructions to jump in line at a grocery store are meant to elicit discomfort and embarrassment. What if we could drop these norms, and jumping when you are inspired to do so could just be experienced and perceived as an expression of joy?

It may be that our perception of social norms has more power than our individual beliefs. In a study of prevalence of recycling, for instance, researchers led by Betsy Levy Paluck, who won a MacArthur "genius grant" for her work on social norms at Princeton University, showed that your opinion of recycling has less to do with whether you believe in the importance of separating cans and newspapers than whether you think most people in your community do it. We are likely to go along with the perceived majority.

When I read that college psychology assignment I just described, it reminded me of my own assignment in which I ask students to create play exercises for adults. As you'll recall, the instructions are these: *Choose one play value that (in your observation) is inaccessible to adults. Design and prototype something to serve this need.* The results promoted silliness and public goofiness as virtues. There was even an elevator intervention (what is it with elevators?), in which my student had occupants sing in exchange for the ride. Several students suggested unexpected physical movement just as the psychology assignment has people jump up and down at the grocery store. All of them encouraged not taking oneself too seriously.

The prohibition on adult play is a social norm worth puncturing. I know this is easier for some than for others. I think being queer and being an artist made my childhood experience of being an outsider even more distinct. From a very early age I knew that social norms were optional. And I was often annoyed with people for following them. Anyone who has questioned their sexuality has let go of societal norms to some extent. We know our lives will look different from most. We either realize the rules are arbitrary or decide we are willing to accept the repercussions of not following them. Perhaps this has something to do with why gay culture is generally more playful than mainstream culture. We've already risked being different and most often experienced judgment because of it. We have broken rules and behaved "wrong" and not just lived to tell the tale—many of us are thriving because of it.

Dance flash mobs are another great example of a healthy violation of social norms. When people in parks or train stations or public plazas suddenly break into hip-hop moves or line dances, it can feel "as unexpected as a snowstorm on a summer's day," wrote dancer and psychologist Peter Lovatt in *The Dance Cure*. Dancing with other people provides a natural high, it stimulates our endogenous opioid systems, and it strengthens positive feelings about our dance partners. That can happen in kitchens, in clubs, at weddings. But the extra fun of dance mobs is the surprise of it. The dancers feel joy, but observers do, too. One video of a flash mob in Antwerp generated tons of positive comments. "This is what the world needs more of," wrote one person. "I wish we could put love and joy back in our daily lives." Sometimes violating social norms is the perfect way to do that.

There are few good reasons for anyone to inhibit their playfulness. And if enough of us question the norm, perhaps we can encourage change not just in ourselves but in society at large. Because in that study about recycling, the researchers also showed that shifting perceptions of social norms may have more influence over behavior change than shifting individual beliefs. According to this way of thinking, a public campaign to increase recycling in a neighborhood would be most effective if it is aimed at telling people "everyone here recycles" rather than "recycling is good." I suppose this book is my effort at a campaign that tells you not only that playing is good for you but also that plenty of adults are doing it.

NEVER ASSUME

Granted, you may have to work at shedding norms. I do, too, in other ways. As a person of a certain age, I try to say yes when invited to activities frequented by those much younger than me. In part I do this because I am curious, and in part because, why not? That's how I ended up at a Day Rave, queuing up on a Brooklyn sidewalk at three on a Saturday afternoon. I go dancing often and had been to this club plenty of times before, but never in daylight. My friends and I had come not from dinner or a bar but from walking dogs, having brunch, running errands. So strange!

We went through a familiar yet now well-lit maze of ticketing and coat checks and entered the club to find giant skylights—sunshine filtering through huge tropical leaves and plants overhead.

We joined the crowd of bobbing heads and swaying bodies as a hypnotic bass filled the space. It was the same as my usual dancing excursions yet kind of unappealing. A fog machine gave the sunlight extra depth. The other dancers are usually anonymous in darkness and lasers, but now we could make eye contact. I had a hard time putting my finger on what was different about it beyond the light, but I just wasn't feeling it. My friends weren't either. At one point, I realized that I was paying so much attention to the differences, I was distracting myself from just having an experience. I was approaching it as a curious observer, an outsider, rather than just letting myself play. That was getting in my way. In artmaking we say, "create first, assess later." I was assessing and reflecting on the play while playing. Once I caught myself doing this, I closed my eyes, bounced a few times, and tuned my attention to the music vibrating through my chest. Even then, my friends and I couldn't get into it. New to the scene, we alienated ourselves, created a crew of "otherness." We decided we hated the rave. My friends went for our coats while I stayed in line for drinks, to go please.

Then something changed. I started chatting with people in line around me and we joked in turn. By the time my friends got back with the coats, I was happy. I introduced everyone and we ended up staying for hours. The whole vibe shifted for us. I was glad I had taken the risk and struck up a conversation, which opened a door to experiencing the rave differently. It was a reminder to be present, to let go of judgment, to just be in the moment.

At its most free, play invites exploration of all sorts. We explore not just what we like to do or the possibility of enjoying a nightclub by day, but who we are. Our identities are flexible when we are young, and we practice that flexibility in play. "Kids say, I can be Mommy, I can be Daddy. I can be the dog," says my friend Tovah Klein, the director of the Barnard College Center for Toddler Development. The many play types that children engage in are also ways of exploring different ways of being. Pretend play is all about this. It is where we learn what it feels like to be both the "good guy" and the "bad guy," to try on identities and get some experience imagining what it might be like to be other kinds of people. As RuPaul says, "we are born naked, and the rest is drag." We practice perceiving ourselves and being perceived as something other than ourselves. We learn empathy. Dressing up as someone else can help us understand ourselves. Sometimes we can fully inhabit some other identity, relishing the opportunity. Other times, it doesn't feel quite right. And we notice that and get some experience imagining what it might feel like to be that other person. What is adolescence but trying on identities? Young people experiment with who they want to be—a jock one year, a Goth the next.

Just as the things I design are open-ended in terms of what they invite players to create, they are open-ended—and open-minded—in the identities they invite players to explore. When we design for a type of play rather than a type of child, we give children the chance to freely explore new stories and activities without preconceived notions of who they are, what they like to do, or what they can become. When adults think in the same way for themselves, they open a world of possibilities. Even though I'm super high energy, it turns out I can sit still and enjoy attention play. And I know a suburban mom, for example, who went to Burning Man with her stepmother. Because why not? Sometimes the only way to break out of our stale ideas of who we can be is to see someone else showing the way.

CREATE FIRST, ASSESS LATER

When I'm designing, I spend a fair amount of time inviting my inner critic to please leave the room. That inner critic includes my Adult Voice telling me I should play it safe and follow every playground code like I'm supposed to. It's also peppered with internalized voices policing social norms: You're too weird, why would anyone pay anyone with messy hair and dirty nails? And of course, there is perhaps the most menacing part of my inner critic, the voice of crippling self-doubt. I admit this now freely, because in doing so in talks over the years, I have met the excitement of recognition—people seem almost elated because they have similar struggles but didn't have the words to describe them.

To silence that persistent inner voice, I begin by clarifying my goals. If I'm in the ideation (brainstorming by sketching) phase, my goal is to find as many ideas as I can, to exhaust all possibilities. When my inner critic chimes in to tell me that my sketches are indecipherable or to point out that *the child in that sketch has a potato foot and amoeba hands*, I remind myself that beautiful illustrations are not the goal.

Second, I give things a time limit. If I am on a roll, then by all means, I go beyond the time, but a set time is a simple way to reassure the voice that wants me to stay on track and be productive with my efforts. I also define for myself what, exactly, I'll be assessing when I'm done creating. What metrics am I using to decide if it's successful? In early stages, the goal is to have *a ton of ideas.* I don't assess based on whether they are feasible or novel or within budget. That happens later, in development. Establishing such parameters early on helps assuage the inner critic's concerns and this pestering companion becomes far less disruptive.

Remember, your inner critic wants to protect you. Whether you're giving a toast at a dinner party, creating art, or preparing a work presentation, be aware of its motives, thank it for its concern, and then invite it to leave the room.

LANGUAGE IS PLAYFUL

Too often, judgment starts with language. Words can be a straitjacket. On the other hand, language gives us all sorts of ways to come at life without baked-in bias. Words can stretch your thinking. Put another way, language is a filter that either opens us up or closes us off to other people, other experiences, other ideas.

When I was rethinking playgrounds, I changed up the language and labels we were using to allow more space for creativity. And I have found that words and labels matter with products like Rigamajig, too. The poster of parts that comes with each set used to describe round pieces as "wheels." But when I visited classrooms, I saw kids imagine that piece as a beehive and then a cookie and then a bee cookie. So newer versions of Rigamajig include shapes that look a lot less like a wheel and are simply called SHAPE 1 and SHAPE 2. Shapes that lend themselves to being a face could also be an animal or grass or mountains. I'm careful not to define the thing by naming it. The shape formerly known as an S Hook lends itself to holding things, as well as representing a tail, or a walking cane, or a snake. If I name it S Hook, what becomes of all those other characters? SHAPE 3 it is.

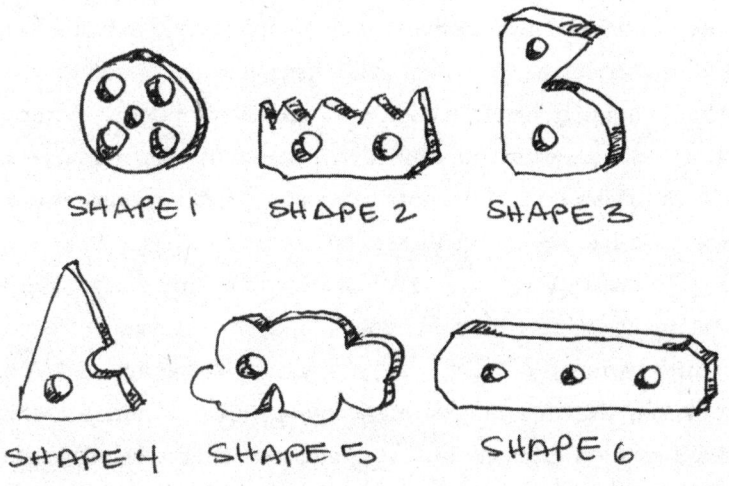

SHAPE 1   SHAPE 2   SHAPE 3

SHAPE 4   SHAPE 5   SHAPE 6

Dr. Seuss's delicious rhyming nonsense words are one way we show children how playful language can be. Not that they need us to tell them. When babies babble and try out making different letter sounds—*ma, ba, ta*—they are experimenting through playing with sound. All through life, we play when we tell jokes, when we create word games, when we think up clever puns and plays on words, when we rap and rhyme. The musical *Hamilton* was celebrated as groundbreaking in large part because of the deft word play and satisfying rhythm and sophistication in the lyrics. Poetry is language play as well as a chance to pause and reflect. It is sometimes open-ended, and sometimes has multiple interpretations, but is often playful.

Even just conversing can be playful if done in the right spirit. I recognize that some people don't speak until they know exactly what they want to say. That can come from a desire to be careful or from worry about how you'll be perceived. My approach is different: I let my words do that work for me. I sometimes say I use "larva language" when I'm using words to play and explore. With a willing friend or collaborator, I'll use conversation to figure out what I think. It is iterative for me. Like an actor doing improv, it is far more playful (and conducive to relational harmony) to say "yes, and" instead of "no, but." If we adopt that approach, we will find ourselves saying yes more often to more things.

For everyone, questions are a way of framing a conversation that makes it playful. Someone with a playful mindset is constantly asking, "What if . . . ?" or saying, "I wonder . . ." "What if we skip dinner and go straight to the show?" "I wonder where that bus goes. Let's get on." I never regret interactions that start with "What if." The question is an especially useful way to rethink priorities, to let go of judgment about what you think you *should* be doing. What if . . . I could spend the next hour . . . day . . . week doing exactly what I chose? What would that be? What would I find fun right now? What's stopping me?

That's how I met Garrett, the colleague who played with his boss on that Wyoming horse fence. We met when we were both on a panel speaking to the board of trustees of the Museum of Modern Art in New York. As the day of discussion wrapped up, there was time to kill before a happy hour with the trustees uptown. I took a bit of a risk and asked Garrett if he wanted to head outside with me and just meander. He was game and before we had gone more than a few blocks, I recognized a kindred spirit. We had been inside all day, being serious with board members, performing adult "play experts." We needed to shake that off; we needed to play. *What if* was second nature to both of us. *What if* we walk to the river? *What if* we hop on a Citi Bike? *I wonder* what we'll see. We ended up riding fifty blocks up the East River, learning about each other's lives, loves, previous bike adventures. We ultimately arrived at the cocktail party sweaty and happier than I'd been in weeks. We paused to "straighten up" in a grand mirror in the lobby, new pals.

The flip side of playful language is linguistic ruts. I recently read an article listing the phrases that couples' therapists wish people would stop using with their significant others. "You always" or "You never" (exaggerated). "You're overreacting" (dismissive). There were more, all of them sadly familiar. These linguistic ruts don't just get laid down in our romantic relationships; they show up in every facet of our lives. To break out of them requires recognizing them in the first place. Do you hear yourself? Is that what you meant to say? Are you relying on old assumptions?

Even the word "play" comes with built-in assumptions. My colleague at the International Training Centre of the International Labour Organization (ITCILO), Tom Wambeke, told me about how he handles this. The ITCILO is a part of the United Nations concerned with training and retraining workers from countries all over the world, as well as keeping an eye on labor conditions and keeping growth opportunities local. For example, in an effort to extend social protection to migrant workers in Africa, the

ITCILO developed a tool kit for outreach workers to better assess the need for aid, and more effectively offer it. Tom is the chief of Learning Innovation at the ITCILO and says that among other things, play helps facilitate communication in groups with multiple languages. It is inclusive, emphasizing soft skills and collaboration. But Tom does have to be careful to introduce the word "play" in the UN context. "People have issues because there are so many connotations," he says. Sometimes he uses the term "gamification," because it doesn't suggest children in the same way. "If we call it gamification, it's not an issue," he says. (I've watched that trend with interest. "Gamification" is a euphemism for "play," one that seems to make it okay for adults, just as the word "recreation" does.)

Tom uses play internally, too. In a recent meeting, several African organizations the ITCILO was working with gathered in Côte d'Ivoire to develop a strategy document. Tom found that various factions in the group had very different ideas of what should be done. There was tension there as everyone got stuck in "rational thinking" and the specificity of the words they were putting on the page. Play let them take a step back. Tom presented them with some recycled materials and asked the group, split into four smaller groups, to model their ideas in three dimensions. "I asked them to build their vision." The catch: No talking, at least not at the beginning. "The tensions that were there went away because they saw different perspectives," Tom says. "They came up with four completely different constructions, but the fact that some of the underlying patterns were the same helped create a real dialogue. People didn't get stuck anymore into their preconceived ideas or language. The communication expert uses this one, the legal expert uses this one. Play became a tool to access a common language."

Another way to get unstuck is to take a lesson from narrative therapy. The stories we tell ourselves *about* ourselves—why we do what we do, what we're good at or bad at—matter. This kind of counseling helps people get some distance from any difficulties they face by having them step back and tell a new story about it. They can "rewrite" their own lives. An older woman, who grew up in the 1940s, remembers being tormented by a teacher who insisted she write with her right hand, even though she was left-handed. In her memory of that year, she was a failure. What if you see yourself as a hero, as a child who survived cruelty? a narrative therapist would ask. To someone who constantly expresses anxiety about getting work accomplished yet never missed a deadline, a therapist might say, What if you told yourself, I am someone who gets things done? What if you started there?

In the same vein, I could ask, What might change if you told yourself: I am a person who plays. What if you started there? I wonder how you might spend the next ten minutes or two hours or next Saturday? If we allow ourselves to believe that play is already part of our lives, it becomes easier to access.

Telling stories more broadly—about the world—is a great way to do that. People have been telling each other stories for thousands of years. Stories help human beings feel in control of a situation, they help us make meaning and find patterns. They also inform our emotional lives when they reveal the differences in how people think. Studies have shown that being a good storyteller benefits an individual; people like to hang out with anyone who can spin a yarn and storytellers receive more social status and rewards. In hunter-gatherer societies, good storytellers are even more likely to have healthy offspring, a fundamental goal of evolution. But having a good storyteller around also benefits a group—their presence is associated with increased cooperation in a community. Anthropologists conclude that it may be that one of the adaptive functions of storytelling in hunter-gatherer societies is to organize the group to work together.

Perhaps that's why so many forms of adult play—accepted forms—involve stories. Books. Film. Theater. Dance. Music. In the spirit of free play, all these arts can be enjoyed spontaneously rather than with a lot of planning. You can change up the genre you usually read on a whim. Or attend a performance specifically because it's the kind of thing you wouldn't usually do. High-brow, low-brow, it's all good. Think of it as playtesting storytelling, of opening up possibilities *and* releasing judgment. What's the worst that could happen? You don't finish the book or you leave at intermission.

FLATTENING HIERARCHIES

Beginning with such an open attitude is key to truly releasing judgment. Open-ended play lets us relax. It lets us drop the need to be grown-up, to be in control, and let go of our worries about what we're good at and what we're not. It also allows adults to collaborate in ways we aren't always used to. Typically, we join forces with someone who has a skill that differs from ours, and we both use our practiced skill. When I collaborate with a wood-worker to make a toy, I worry about how it will be played with, and they worry about how it's built. But in play our priorities aren't so linear, so our specific skill set may not be the point. And there can be lovely benefits to treating everyone as an equal contributor on all fronts.

Sometimes corporations seek the out-of-the-box thinking that art and design students can bring. In that spirit, I once ran a collaborative research class with RISD students and the team at Samsung who work on flat-screen televisions. Samsung was interested in innovating their products and they were asking what the future of flat screens would be. In the class, we took a step back (Name-by-Function again) and rethought the goal by asking not just about flat screens but about home entertainment as a concept. *What does it mean to be entertained?* We changed the design brief to "Future Scenarios in Living Spaces" and explored how technology can help households play together. We wanted to have people shift from consuming entertainment to participating in it. (Read: not just watching TV.) The class included students from five different art disciplines—e.g., apparel, fine arts, etc.— each with rather specific skill sets. The undefined outcome of the assignment meant no one skill set carried more importance than any other and led to a nonhierarchical collaboration within the groups. It meant the students could really play together. The end projects showed this. For instance, one spread technology around to engage an entire living room instead of just the television and the sofa.

The designers at Samsung embraced the possibilities we came up with and the senior executive involved was excited and open to these innovative and playful approaches to future products. But as I continued working with them, we realized that they also had to rethink the corporate structure if these ideas were really going to be explored—their hierarchy did not lend itself to green-lighting ideas that strayed that far from their existing technologies. To be radically innovative, whole companies need to be willing to embrace possibility, release judgment, and reframe success.

An example of a corporate structure that tackles the trouble with hierarchies is Honda—at least in one way, the *waigaya*. Company lore holds that Takeo Fujisawa, the business partner of founder Soichiro Honda, invented the *waigaya*, sessions designed to flatten hierarchy and, therefore, spur innovative thinking. *Waigaya* isn't a word in Japanese. Fujisawa thought it sounded like many people talking at the same time, kind of like "hubbub" in English. These gatherings can be called at any moment and are held outside of conference rooms. (Even utility closets have become spaces for brainstorming.) According to Jeffrey Rothfeder, author of *Driving Honda: Inside the World's Most Innovative Car Company*, the four tenets of *waigaya* are the following:

1. All are equal and can speak with impunity.

2. Debate on every idea continues until it is either proven valid or rejected.

3. Once an idea is shared, it belongs to the group.

4. At the end of the session, participants generate a clear list of who is to do what and by when.

That last tenet is a testament to how seriously Honda takes this process. This is not a gesture to nonhierarchy. This is the real deal.

To be clear, some of these meetings lead nowhere and that is okay. Soichiro Honda once said, "Success is ninety-nine percent failure." But *waigaya* have become so ingrained in company culture that there is a long list of examples of these meetings producing the way forward. The one that got held in a closet at a plant in Ohio, for example, generated a simple solution to a potentially expensive manufacturing problem when a quality-control expert remembered a detail from an earlier plant visit that resulted in a cheaper, faster fix than the original plan. A playful mindset is what makes this kind of thing work. *Waigaya* uses open-endedness, a lack of hierarchy, language, and lingering in the What if . . . As Honda says on its website, doing nothing through fear of failure prevents progress. They celebrate "getting rid of 'no play, no errors.'"

You don't have to be a multinational corporation to benefit from *waigaya*. I could see this working anywhere that a power dynamic could change how able and willing people are to hear each other's ideas.

In that Nike workshop I led, playing together allowed the employees to release judgment about their own performance. Since there were so many ways to contribute and succeed in the prompt, they also released judgment about each other, about whose ideas mattered. Assistants didn't have to disappear into the background. Bosses didn't have to be right. Athletes didn't have a built-in advantage. It was an opportunity for everyone to let down their guard, to see each other in a new light and appreciate the possibilities and humanity that each person displayed.

That flattening of hierarchy allows for a complexity of understanding. It allows for more voices and better ideas. It lets everyone contribute. "If we don't include our associates in the decision-making, we're ignoring potentially our most valuable asset," a Honda plant manager told Rothfeder. When you remove hierarchy, you see people as individuals rather than as a receptionist or a CEO. Our identities are more than what we do in the dynamics formed at work.

What a helpful reminder of the value of letting go of judgment, both of yourself and of others. Play gets us to that state in a way that few other activities do. And once we let go of judgment, play lets us explore ourselves, our identities, our possibilities. We don't have to draw conclusions or form opinions. We don't have to worry about blending in or standing out. It's time away from worrying about what we got done or what we said or why the world is the way it is. The world will still be waiting, after all. And some time spent in judgment-free play can help us return to it with fresh energy and enthusiasm.

7

REFRAME SUCCESS

E milia Richeson has always loved dancing. As a child of the '80s she'd particularly loved aerobics, and, well into adulthood, dreamed of leading her own class. To actually do it, though, she'd have to overcome her fear of not being thin enough or cheerful enough and get past feeling intimidated by fitness culture and all its trappings. A friend of hers was aware of her dream and took on the role of playworker for her—he rented a space, told her to prepare music and moves, and rallied a few friends to show up ready to follow her lead. She regularly says that friend gave her "an incredible gift" by setting up a low-stakes environment where she could "try it on" and playtest her dream.

From there she led classes at a few gyms, and eventually founded Pony Sweat Aerobics. Her mission: "A fiercely non-competitive dance aerobics practice. We celebrate anti-perfectionism and freedom of movement." The format of most dance exercise classes (think Jazzercise or Zumba) is lead-follow. For the participants, success looks like emulating the teacher, both in how the moves are done, and less explicitly, in what their bodies look like. Uniformity is the goal. In a Pony Sweat class, there is still a leader because leaders provide tangible, physical prompts. But people can follow or not follow. Success, Emilia told me, is when participants "feel they have nothing to achieve, they follow curiosity and desire." She helps them get there by giving permission. "I tell them to trust themselves, play with their movements, and remind them to fuck the moves!" Following Emilia's lead doesn't mean duplicating her moves; it means exploring movement and being in the moment. That last bit, *fuck the moves*, is Emilia's mantra. It means: Don't worry about the steps. Mess them up. Ignore them. Riff on them. Exercise is a by-product of the play, not the point.

After a few classes with her, I can attest to the joy of the experience. I fucked the moves firsthand. When I was lost in the spins and kicks, the sea of bodies around me—all shapes and sizes in every variety of sweatpants and crop tops and leotards—laughed with me, whether they were on beat or as lost as I was. And that was the point: to sweat (there was plenty), to laugh (also an abundance), and to find joy in embodied play. As always, dancing together helped us feel connected. And all that movement got our blood pumping and stimulated our brains.

Much of what we do as adults—and as children—is focused on "success." And success is almost always understood and measured by outcomes. It's right there in the definition of the word: "a favorable or desired outcome." For adults, that outcome often has to do with money or status or achievement of some kind. Success is dictated by external rewards and extrinsic motivation. If we sing, we should sing well. At school, we should get good grades. In sports like running or cycling, we should cover distance or better our previous time. If we write a book, it should sell lots of copies. (Thank you for buying this one.)

But you don't have to "succeed" in traditional ways to enjoy an activity or to have it be worth doing. If it brings you joy or stokes your curiosity or connects you to someone, those are successes, too. Who cares if you're not great, or even good, at something if you enjoy the experience or no one sees you do it? If you take up ceramics because you love the feel of the clay, so what if you throw a lopsided pot? If you ice a birthday cake yourself, all the better if the flowers look like dead leaves! Of course, these are small ventures compared to some of the big risks we take on, like starting a business or a relationship. But even there, I'd argue that failure can be an essential ingredient to a fuller, more holistic idea of success. And all of them require bravery and trusting that those around you won't judge the outcome but admire the effort.

This is why the third and final element of free play for adults is reframing success. If you want to explore, you must be willing to get lost. If you want to create something new, you must travel somewhere new in your thinking. That means being willing to test approaches that might not work and looking to learn from them. It means rethinking the goal of an activity and what you aim to get from it. It means being in it for yourself, for the experience, no matter how the outside world responds. Play is the perfect place to do all that. It's a safe place where we can focus on process not product, where failure is part of the fun, and risk is its own reward. Taking a new approach—at any age—requires intention. It's a reminder of Penny Wilson's definition of "free play" as something that is freely chosen, personally directed, and intrinsically motivated. For an adult, that means unpacking purpose, embracing complexity and the possibility of failure. It means recognizing that not everything will work out as we imagine. And being okay with that.

FAILURE IS NOW AN OPTION

I launched my own toy company so I could design and produce the kind of toys I wanted to see in the world—that was Geemo, initially. Running my own company meant using all kinds of skills that didn't come naturally to me (i.e., I'm bad at), like bookkeeping. I read *Entrepreneurship for Dummies* and *The Toy and Game Inventor's Handbook*. I listened intently to business advice from anyone who would give it. I convinced friends to spend their Saturdays teaching me how to build a website (in 2006 it was a pain in the ass) and how to make proper spreadsheets. "Excel is the tool of the new revolution!" I proclaimed, partly to convince myself this was worth doing. If I could keep the business afloat, I would change the world one open-ended toy at a time.

In the discourse around businesses and founders, we talk about success as growth. Since mine was a toy company, I assumed that to be successful, I was meant to grow—to develop more products, manage employees, accumulate more distributors, and sell more toys, and from all of that, make a profit. The assumption behind this version of success is that the goal is profits. While the need to support myself is not something I dispute, my goal was to design more great toys. I kept forgetting to prioritize the profit part.

By many standards, Geemo *was* a success—it launched at the MoMA Store in New York City, sold out numerous times in Japan, and garnered me all-expenses-paid travel to Seoul, Tokyo, Moscow, and Hamburg for design festivals. But by business standards, it failed. My margins were minuscule. Geemo was manufactured in a small factory in Japan, where I had a great sales partner who drove the bulk of the sales and did wonderful events and exhibits with it. In the US, I was doing marketing and sales myself, haphazardly. None of my business management library books prepared me for the seemingly endless stream of worst-case scenarios that emerged in succession, each of them hurting sales. There was a news story about a toddler who'd eaten some fridge magnets and nearly died, making all magnetic toys seem terrifying. And I lost an entire shipment of inventory to an overheated shipping container.

When it became clear I couldn't keep going, I was initially despondent. I remembered all the terrible toys I'd seen at various toy fairs. I had a great one. Why couldn't I make it work?! But one day not long after the US economy sank from the 2008 mortgage crisis, I saw a story in the satirical newspaper *The Onion*.

"Failure Now an Option," read the headline.

"1,435,643 instances of failure reported last Sunday alone," read the story.

I whooped with delight. Then I plastered copies of that article all over my studio. I needed to reframe what I considered success.

I needed to let the toy part of my business fail. It would be okay.
What a liberating feeling! No, I had not managed to get my toy
onto the market in an efficient manner and build a collection of
new products or make a lot of money. But I had learned so much.
I had built a foundation of manufacturing and sales experience
that would inform everything I did going forward. I had accumulated new contacts and colleagues, other like-minded designers
and play advocates. I would not have done any of that if I hadn't
bravely pursued something unusual, by myself. I took Geemo off
the market and labeled it "limited edition." But when I created
Rigamajig a few years later, I took it into the market myself . . .
again. I like the saying "you're either winning or learning." With
Geemo, I was failing at profit but winning at learning.

Failure gets a very bad rap in our culture, but plenty of il-
lustrious people have learned from what went wrong, as I did. "I
have not failed," Thomas Edison is reputed to have said about his
efforts to invent a lightbulb. "I have just found 10,000 ways that
didn't work." Agatha Christie's first novel was rejected numerous
times and so was her second, which was only published after she
agreed to change the ending. Yet she went on to write more than
seventy books. James Dyson, whose eponymous vacuum company
is a global phenomenon, made 5,126 prototypes before he created
the first viable bagless vacuum cleaner. In the technology world,
where so many projects come out of start-ups, many top private
equity firms have a bottom-line requirement for the new companies they consider: They won't invest in entrepreneurs who haven't
failed at least three times already.

In play, failure is essential. Few of us manage to skip stones
all the way across the pond on our first try. The joy is in the

continued effort. It is in being by the water, in the feel of a smooth stone in your hand, and the marvel of how many varieties of stones there are to be found on the beach. And maybe there is fun to be had in changing up the goal. What if instead of the best flat stone you can find, you switch to big lumps of rock that are almost certain to sink immediately? Now success could be the biggest *kerplunk* with bonus points if the rock even hints at skipping.

All through life, there should be room to learn from failure, to learn how to build on it, how to recover from it. Alas, we aren't trained that way. It's likely that at some point in your education you found yourself in class—perhaps math or spelling—and had no idea how to solve the problem that everyone else appeared to have finished. Then the classmate who always knew the answer— the star—went to the front of the room and showed off their knowledge. Do you remember how defeated you felt? And did you learn anything other than shame from their demonstration? In Japan, I hear that's not how they do it. It's not the child who knows the answer who goes to the front of the class, it's the child who doesn't know. The child who is struggling to understand goes up front and the whole class helps that child work out the answer—together. By doing this, they are modeling how to figure it out collaboratively. Doing it our way—with the star students doing the demonstrating—means those who struggle don't learn how to do whatever it is they're studying. They just learn they were wrong and end up feeling alone. We learn to hide wrong answers—and don't get a chance to learn from them. Failure is an inevitable and important part of learning. What would it look like to embrace it?

For me, that looks like recognizing all the successful failures in our lives. As I playtest or talk through something, I sometimes find that the design isn't playable, or isn't that interesting in use, or doesn't work from a form or material standpoint. Some designs fail because I can't figure out how to make them affordable. One playground project fell apart because I realized, after too many rounds of pitching great ideas, that the clients didn't trust children. They thought they wanted my kind of design, but when it came to making decisions, they rejected every unconventional idea. I can't work with people who don't trust kids. Now, in my work with museums and corporations, I want it in writing that clients know what they're getting into with me, that they're willing to be brave and willing to have some extra steps and conversations, that they're going to be a good advocate for the work when they go in to get the building permits. The more intentional we are in the foundation of a project, the more creative we can be in designing it.

Curiosity, in its lack of attachment to outcome, welcomes failure. Too often, we become paralyzed by the possibility of not getting something right. Once, as a joke, I switched the language on my mother's cellphone into Spanish. She'd been trying to learn the language so I thought the immersion might help her. (Or that is the story I told her. Really, I'm just a prankster. Or maybe I'm a terrible daughter? Probably both.) I did think it would be easier for her to figure out how to get it back than it was, and that the effort would encourage her to play around with the settings. It did the opposite. The stakes were too high, and the experience made my mom even more afraid to try to figure the phone out once she knew that inadvertently swapping to a whole other language was a possible outcome of experimenting. That kind of fear is not conducive to curiosity. It leads to frustration and tentativeness. (Of course, I changed it back.)

A more playful, curious approach that's unafraid of failure and measures success by a different yardstick would be the Americans I know who go to other countries and throw themselves into trying to speak the language even though they will always sound like they're from Texas or Boston or Minnesota. I know someone who calls that approach "linguistic linguini" for the way he throws words and phrases at the wall to see what sticks. The native speakers he meets seem to appreciate the effort even if they chuckle at his butchering of their language. He laughs right along with them, and he gets something out of his travels that more timid folks miss—trying to speak the language means he is engaging in the place differently, challenging himself, learning. He is curious about the language and the place and the people.

In everything I do, I try to operate at the border between challenge and frustration. Challenge and risk are where learning and growth happen. To hang a swing on my property, I didn't just find an accessible tree branch. I donned a harness and climbed 100 feet into a tree to fix the rope to the perfect branch so that the swing would fall right over the brook.

Seeking that tension between challenge and frustration was how I came up with the precarious stacks at the Liberty Science Center. In a play exhibit I designed for the Queens Museum in New York City, I created a giant, 10 x 20-foot pad of paper with oversized drawing tools that were deliberately awkward to use. The handles were curved and twisted and often wearable, so the children spun, slid, and danced to make marks on the paper surface that unrolled across the floor. I did it that way because inviting people to draw publicly in an art museum can induce anxiety. There's so much beauty around! It can be intimidating. I wanted visitors to experience the fun and playfulness of art without the pressure of it needing to be good. The awkwardness of the tools inspired play, as did the challenge of figuring out how to use them. The joy for children was in using their bodies in new ways and creating something unexpected, from a process that was uncontrollable. Because there was no one way, the kids tried again and again to keep experimenting. They didn't get frustrated. The art left behind was literal traces of play.

Much of what adults do for play doesn't get all that close to challenging—at least not when we only do things that are familiar, that we know we are good at or that keep us in our comfort zone. The saying tells us to dance as if no one is watching, but do you? Like my ex-ballerina friend, we stop doing the thing we love once we get the message—accurate or not—that we are too tall, aren't good enough, or that we don't belong. Too many of us let whatever that thing was slide out of our lives except as spectators even though you could keep dancing, or singing, or playing a sport in a variety of ways and at a variety of levels.

Sometimes we just convince ourselves we won't succeed. We don't invite people to dinner if we are too afraid our cooking won't pass muster. And we think that ordering pizza or arranging a potluck wouldn't be good enough. In whose eyes? Most people are thrilled if someone goes to the trouble of inviting them into their home and bringing them together with other friends. There are so many ways to provide food and drink that do not require you to be Martha Stewart. Why not try them out? Challenge yourself to entertain in the least stressful way possible. What would that look like for you? Just drinks and appetizers? A bagel-centered brunch? A rotating party where guests move from house to house, with each home responsible for a course?

PLAY WITH YOUR OWN RISK

Remember that book about learning everything you really needed to know in kindergarten? I'd argue you could learn everything you really need to know about reframing success from a model of preschools in China. Collectively they embrace a philosophy called Anji Play in which children are allowed to manage their own risks, teachers observe but rarely intervene, and even the goal of a lesson is surprisingly counterintuitive. "What were you curious about?" the teachers ask.

"I tried using sandbags as cushions," a child might answer, "to see what it would be like to jump onto them." That moment of curiosity becomes a discussion for the entire class.

"I tried that once," another child will say. "It was different from jumping onto the mats. It felt like . . ."

What were you curious about is the defining question of Anji Play. Notice it is not "What did you learn?" Shifting the emphasis to curiosity opens up much more inquiry, and leaves room for learning that might not be visible to teachers. It reframes the goal of their pursuits and, therefore, what counts as success for the teachers and the school. In asking "What did you learn?" we imply there needed to be an outcome to work toward. In "What were you curious about?" we emphasize the process, and motivation itself. *What were you curious about* is not measurable in the usual way, and it is a vital question—one adults can ask themselves as well.

Anji is a county in eastern Zhejiang province, about three hours from Shanghai. Lush, green, and shrouded in mist, Anji is most well-known among Westerners as the scene of the iconic sword fight in the swaying bamboo trees in *Crouching Tiger, Hidden Dragon.* In the mid-2000s, Anji also became the scene of a revolutionary approach to early education. A former teacher and principal named Cheng Xueqin was given the job of overseeing curriculum development for the county's 130 public preschools, which serve about 14,000 children aged three to six.

I had never heard of Anji or Ms. Cheng until I got a call out of the blue one day from an American educator, Chelsea Bailey, who had been traveling in China as part of a team consulting with Chinese schools. In the schools in Anji county, Chelsea and her colleagues had repeatedly seen a toy that they soon worked out was a knockoff of Rigamajig. I didn't know Chelsea, but she called and left me a message. She wanted to alert me to the situation but also talk to me about the wonders of Anji Play. At first, I was focused on—and upset by—the fact that someone was copying and selling my design. I have patents to protect from this. You can't just take a toy designed by someone else and produce your own version of it. My business manager wanted to shut them down. He and I went to meet with Chelsea and her colleague, Jesse Coffino, who'd recently started working with Anji Play schools. They told me, "We're sorry you're being knocked off, but you have to see what is going on in these schools." Then Chelsea opened her laptop and showed us pictures of Anji Play.

I saw a playground full of children climbing up a hodgepodge of hand-built wooden and rope structures, walking on top of rolling barrels, leaping off ladders. It was like looking at a yard full of Rube Goldberg devices, those cartoon chain-reaction machines that shuttle balls through obstacle courses. There was not one linear path in the bunch. Each construction rose, fell, turned, and twisted with the imagination of the children who had built it. I had never seen anything like it.

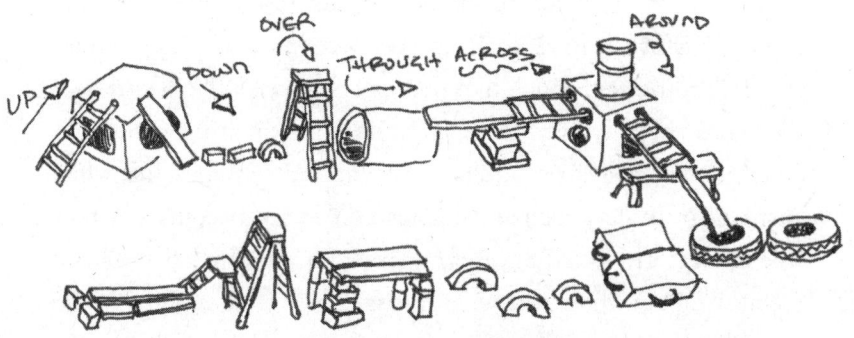

"What am I looking at?" I asked them in wonder.

Chelsea started telling me about Ms. Cheng, a woman on a mission. The Rigamajig knockoff came about because Ms. Cheng had seen pictures of Rigamajig in magazines but couldn't buy it in China. So, she found a factory to make her own. She had not really intended to steal my intellectual property; she just wanted her children to have Rigamajig or something close to it.

When Ms. Cheng first took over, early education in Anji looked much like it did elsewhere in China. Young children were encouraged to sit quietly at their desks for most of the day. Looking around classrooms, Ms. Cheng was troubled by that. She had recently read the United Nations 1989 Convention on the Rights of the Child, which states, among other things, that children have the right to rest and leisure, and "to engage in play and recreational activities appropriate to the age of the child." That idea—that play is fundamental to children's experience and learning—resonated with Ms. Cheng. But in the classrooms under her charge, she saw no play. There was no joy, either.

To reintroduce play as a foundational activity, she began by recalling her own memories of play as a young child, as well as eliciting those of other teachers and administrators. A theme emerged: Most people's early memories were defined by risk and self-determination. Much like the play memories I've heard over the years, they involved children building or creating something on their own, away from adults and organized activities, like when cushions from the couch are arranged on-end to become a fort, or tree stumps are rolled around as props for jumping. Ms. Cheng recognized childhood for what it was, a rare time of life. "If the children in our care have this one unique moment of childhood in their lives," she asked, "why are we stripping away the joy and discovery that is so essential to it?"

Her solution: rethinking the goal and structure of preschool entirely. If kids want to be outside all day, why are we working against that? Ms. Cheng made the outdoors as important as the indoors. What we would call the playground is the beating heart of each school. The kids spend one-third of their day outside, but it isn't recess. The playground is an open-ended, child-directed classroom. It's not a break from the learning—it is learning.

Those playgrounds are large, minimally structured, open-ended areas full of large, minimally structured materials, such as ladders, barrels, giant wooden cubes, planks, and sandbags filled with flaxseed (large enough to be awkward, but light enough for children to pick up and move). The abundance of playthings is astonishing. Teachers let children work things out for themselves. They let them resolve conflicts and let them assess how much risk they can handle. Can they jump from 6 feet up? How about 10?

Children take out whatever they think would be interesting to play with on any given day. They make elaborate obstacle courses out of the materials at hand—giant ladders, huge boxes, barrels, mats. The courses evolve and grow as the kids work on them, increasing the level of challenge as kids are ready for it. There is a palpable intensity to the children's activities. They might roll on a barrel or inside a barrel, from there climb a ladder, crawl across another ladder laid horizontally to connect to a separate platform, then climb a few more rungs to a higher level, and finally jump from a height. As soon as they finish a challenge, they add to it and change it. In one creation, they set it up so that a tire bounced down a ladder. Then they tried to time it so that planks on both sides moved to guide the tire. When they got that part to work, they celebrated briefly. Then they kept building and stretching their obstacle course to take over more of the yard. The principle at work is the same one that makes video games so addictive. As soon as you get good, you level up and take on something harder. Because once you solve a puzzle, you don't really want to do it again.

In Anji Play, children manage their own risk. They work up to jumping from higher heights. The materials include thick mats of dense foam, and kids decide how many mats to lay down at the base of the jump and how far to set them from the platform. Their expertise comes from the collective experience. They learn from one another. Three-year-old children see the fours and fives working with larger challenges and know one day they'll use the eight-rung ladder, too. In the meantime, they have the two-rung ladder to contend with.

One of the highest jumps is known as "the courage log." I watched a girl sit up at the top of it—maybe 10 or 12 feet off the ground—for most of an outdoor session. There was a teacher with her the whole time, just standing by. The girl had already jumped from all the lesser heights, and she was ready for this one, but she took her time. For a while, she just seemed to be hanging out up there. Periodically, a friend would climb partway up the log and say something encouraging or just tell her a story from the other side of the playground. The teacher chimed in to say she didn't have to jump if she didn't want to. But when she finally did jump, no one made a big deal of it and the girl walked away as if it was all unremarkable. In a very real sense, it was. She had known she could do it and that she would succeed eventually, on her own terms.

In most of the world, adults tell children that it isn't safe to turn a barrel on its side and walk on top of it. You'll slip. You'll fall. You'll get hurt. Adults also say that ladders allow them—and only them—to reach tall places. But balancing on ladders and walking along rolling barrels is play in Anji. And furthermore, every parent with a child at an Anji Play school is required to come walk on the barrels and climb the ladders themselves at the start of the school year. That's partly so they understand what their children are doing all day but it's also to remind the adults in a not-so-subtle way of the joys of play, of the fun to be had in taking risks and challenging yourself.

Some adults are all-in on risk in play and go skydiving or bungee jumping. That's certainly one way to do it. But there's emotional risk in less physical activities. When something is new or an activity you rarely engage in—dancing at a wedding or doing a turkey trot run—you can't know at the start how it will go. People are desperately afraid of looking foolish. I went recently to a puppet show that involved fifty volunteers and I could tell most of them weren't used to being onstage. Some of them were clearly nervous, even terrified. They were risking embarrassment or feeling responsible for the success of the show. But the show was built around the voluntary nature of its performers, and I loved every minute of it. As an audience member, I saw the joy the performers brought to the show, as well as their nervousness. It brought *me* joy to see these adults playing onstage.

What is risky for adults is not the same as what is risky for children. Sometimes it flips. It's natural for a child to get up onstage with puppets. For an adult who is not a performer, it can be crippling. For a small child, jumping off a 3-foot ladder is risky. For most adults, that's not a big deal. Children change their minds every week about what they want to do when they grow up. Firefighter then zookeeper then ballerina then ballerina/novelist. Adults find the thought of changing jobs paralyzing. There might be real financial risk in it (i.e., a pay cut or restarting at a lower level), and some may feel shame, as if they made a mistake in their first career choice.

We adults are risk-averse because we have narrowed what we do based on what we're good at. That limits our options for fun as well as for work. As the Zen master Shunryū Suzuki once said, "In the beginner's mind there are many possibilities, but in the expert's there are few." The fear of risk can be offset by playtesting your way into it, whether it is a new hobby or interest or side hustle. If we tackle the hard things through play, some of that attitude rubs off on the rest of our lives. And we might be more willing to let go of fear and meet challenges head-on, even if the tools are awkward and we have to roll around to figure out how to use them.

ENGAGE IN CURIOUS LOOKING

How can you let go of fear? One way is to actively think about how you look at the world—both objects and experiences. Step back. Shut one eye. Stand on one leg or maybe even lie down. Do things look different? Do you see an opportunity where before you saw an obstacle? Instead of looking sideways, you could simply look with curiosity. As Corita Kent's frames for looking remind us, so much of our perspective depends on the way we view the world. It's playful to commit to looking in fresh new ways and being willing to see differently. That might mean physically changing your approach—bending to see something from below, climbing up high to look down, squinting, looking at less. Zooming in, zooming out. Or it might mean being aware of the associations and assumptions you have with the things you are looking at (like barrels and ladders). A literal reframing can help get us to a new way of thinking; it can help us go deeper.

Ms. Cheng didn't stand on her head to rethink preschools, but she might as well have. She shifted her priorities, redefining the driving goals of preschools, to construct children's days around curiosity and well-being. To do that, she prioritized play.

Some of her rethinking had to do with objects. What's brilliant about the Anji Play materials is that they are intentionally humble and mundane. They offer a different way of looking at everyday things—a reminder that play is everywhere. Those ladders are the same ladders you find on construction sites in China. The bamboo baskets are the same baskets that laundry is stored in at home. The barrels are the same as barrels all over the cities and towns of Anji County.

Adults are so used to seeing objects like these as having one function, we tend not to see their possibilities. By appropriating (or "misusing") those everyday materials for play, Ms. Cheng's schools tell us play is everywhere and just about anything can be transformed into something that's challenging and fun. As a bonus, Ms. Cheng's approach gives her students agency in the adult world. I imagine them going around their towns and cities with their big people. They spot baskets, buckets, and ladders while we adults continue being our serious selves with them. And the kids think, *I know what to do with that. I can handle that ladder. You're not so special.* The world becomes less overwhelmingly huge and unknown. They belong.

Adults can learn to look differently at the everyday, too. We can see the cardboard box as construction material and not just a container. We can see the whiteboard as a sketch pad and not just a to-do list. I say "see" but we can apply the same approach to our thinking and to our other senses beyond vision. We can listen with playful attention. On your next walk leave your headphones behind. Without music or podcasts to listen to, you can make a game of listening to what you hear. Whether you're in a city, a forest, or somewhere in between, there is a lot to engage with our senses. Attention play. Multiple languages, people joking, squirrels yelling at each other, trees creaking, adults explaining things to dogs and children, birds singing . . . A friend recently did this and was so captivated by the range of humanity she'd heard that she went home and wrote it up as a poem—something she had not done since college, when writing poetry was an assignment.

We can touch or move with attention. Engage in some thinkering, using your hands to help you think. Draw a line on a page, a squiggle, or a circle, and then turn it into something, see what it wants to become. Dig in the dirt, with your hands. Run your fingers through some sand or buy yourself some Play-Doh just for the sensory pleasures of kneading it. Touch things you habitually avoid. Is it raining? Ditch the umbrella and let yourself get wet. There's a reason kids love to jump in puddles in their boots. Let yourself have that kind of moment of glee. Clothes and hair dry. We, too, can be playful and creative in how we get what we need from our surroundings. When was the last time you allowed yourself the time needed to take on a challenge, just for the fun of it? When was the last time you climbed a ladder not to change a lightbulb or clean the gutter but to simply change your perspective on the world? Ladders are perfect for that. They are a great way to get up close to the leaves in the trees or to reach the roof for a hangout. If you happen to be one who clears your gutters, don't climb down right away. A roof, like my childhood tree, is a great perch to watch the world from a new viewpoint.

You can change your perspective and stay on the ground, too. A team of psychologists once set up a study in which they had some people walk around the perimeter of a room and others walk freely around the middle. When they later tested everyone's creativity, those who had walked freely scored higher. I have no idea if that study has been replicated, but it speaks to the value of avoiding predictability. I'm a big fan of collaborators Arakawa and Gins. They designed spaces, from buildings to parks, that intentionally avoided predictability—playing with surfaces, levels, corners, edges. In one of their houses, you have to pay close attention to move around safely. It demands your full presence. Such active engagement with your surroundings was the essence of being alive, they thought. They called their work "architecture against death."

You don't have to go that far in your own life. Try changing up the way you move around your office or go to the grocery store. Peter Lovatt, the psychologist who encourages us to always be dancing, suggests taking the stairs in your house as if you were on the set of an MGM musical or as if you were Rocky Balboa preparing for the title bout. Be extra once in a while!

Sometimes curious looking becomes a whole game in its own right. I was once on a road trip across Italy with a family of four, dear friends of mine, when a predictable fussiness began to set in. There was teenage angst, traffic, and general boredom to contend with. I was gazing out the window in the back seat with the kids, when we stopped in front of a Gothic cathedral. Its gargoyles glared down at me. I heard myself narrating their judgment of our state: "What's wrong with you humans in your precious metal boxes on wheels, sitting miserably for hours?" I giggled a little, then decided to voice the gargoyle's question to the group. The tension broke and the whole family jumped in. "My shift is over. When is Benedict going to clock in so I can go eat a cat?" We had taken curious looking and added fantastical storytelling to it. We stopped noticing the traffic and started noticing opportunities to tell tales. The game lifted the teenager out of her grouch. And no one was bored anymore. We played for the rest of the road trip and the family plays the game to this day, bringing to life (and voice) the characters built into the architecture around them. Attention and creative play.

PLAY WITH PROCESS

We can also change our perspective by focusing on the experience rather than on the end result. They do that at Anji Play every day in multiple ways. My favorite is cleanup. Watching it blows my mind every time. One child walks around the playground with a radio playing music to signal that the time has come. But there's no immediate rush. The tenor and enthusiasm of the students don't change. Instead, in time, pieces begin migrating back to where they started the day. When I say there's no rush, I mean it. The Anji Play system includes specially designed pedal carts that the children use for playing and moving materials. During one cleanup session, I watched a five-year-old devise a slow but steady system. She put one block on each pedal of her cart, stood atop them, and maneuvered her way to the storage area, up, down, up, down, pedaling her blocks across the yard. She placed them where they belonged, all two of them, then pedaled back to the pile she was working from and placed two more blocks under her feet. Eventually, everyone else had gone inside and this girl was still slowly, methodically moving two blocks at a time across the yard. It was fascinating but also frustrating to observe, like being stuck behind a vintage tractor on a country road. The impulse to just move things along can be strong (yes, I am a fast-walking New Yorker).

"When do you tell her, enough, speed it up?" I asked the teacher who was waiting for the girl to finish.

She looked at me in what I took to be genuine surprise. "Why would I do that?" she asked. "What can she learn inside that she's not learning here? Why is that more important than this?"

Oh wow. It was an aha moment for me—one that helped explain why Anji Play was so radical. It's about priorities.

Why is that more important than this?

Anji Play has reordered the hierarchy of importance, calling the whole edifice into question. It is the question we need to ask ourselves if we are going to let go of preconceived notions of success and purpose. Mostly we do think one thing is more important than another. Certainly, we think many things outrank play. Why is *that*—be it work, chores, seriousness—more important than play? That list of priorities represents our Adult Voice talking (and underestimating play). In this case, frankly, our Play Voice, that one that's been with us since childhood, the one that prompts us to run outside and roll down the hill, knows better.

Yet so much of our lives are structured around the things we think—or society tells us are most important. Productivity, efficiency, work, family or romance over friends, chores over childishness. To that I say: Take a risk. Push yourself. By definition, learning is moving beyond what you already know. But sometimes we forget to keep learning when we're busy "succeeding" in the realms we have already conquered. That's where success is easiest.

If we're willing to reframe success, we can push ourselves to experiment beyond our comfort zone—that might mean reorganizing your daily schedule, it might mean rearranging the furniture, or it might mean going back to school or taking a leap into a new career.

There's also value in listening to your Play Voice, the one I talked about earlier. I guarantee your Play Voice has a different idea of success than your Adult Voice. It sees the glory in kneading bread and doesn't worry about the evenness of the finished crust. It sees the fun in finger painting even if some blue paint gets under your nails and sees the purpose in piling up pillows to make a fort that will have to come down again soon. Your Play Voice values something other than the result. It is focused on experience, on joy, on your psychic well-being. We can listen to the voice in our head that suggests an unpredictable use for something. We can ignore the voice that tells us no, stick to the norm. We can listen to the voice that tells us we loved singing in a group and ignore the voice passing judgment on whether we were in tune. We can listen to the voice that tells us trying is its own form of success, that doing is its own form of success, and that where we end up doesn't matter so much. And ignore everything else for a little while.

WHAT ARE YOU AFTER?

The fact that I was there in China watching that little girl pedal across the yard during cleanup was a result of my own version of reframing success. Instead of suing Ms. Cheng for patent infringement, I collaborated with her. After getting past the shock of it and taking a timeout with my ego, I asked myself what I was trying to do with Rigamajig. Yes, I wanted (and needed) to earn a living. And yes, I was proud of my work and felt ownership of it. But my true goal was to have an impact on play and education, to give kids an opportunity to build giant things without instructions. Kids everywhere. That's exactly what was happening. Why would I shut it down? I needed to rethink what success looked like in this instance. It wasn't only my business profiting from the use of my ideas; it was children around the world benefiting from it. That was the goal.

When I decided to check out Anji Play for myself, I flew to China, met Ms. Cheng, and we hit it off. We resolved some of the business issues. The company that had been making the fake Rigamajig agreed to pay me a licensing fee. And then Ms. Cheng hired me to standardize the playground materials that her schools were using. The Anji Play model was expanding further afield in China and the local carpenters making the required ladders and barrels were straining to keep up. Because there was no single set of drawings or plans, the system had a dizzying number of variations of each item with many local differences, as if a franchise fast-food restaurant tweaked its menu in every new town.

The process illuminated how much I still had to learn about play. Our effort started with streamlining the ladders. They had thirty-seven versions. I was trying to get the total number of variations down to about twelve. In my first design review meeting with Ms. Cheng, I pointed to a photo of two ladders in use in a school. It seemed obvious to me that here was an instance where there could be one ladder instead of two.

"They're the same height," I said. "One has rungs that are

eighteen inches apart, and the other has rungs that are twelve inches apart. One is made of bamboo and one of pine; we need to choose one material and one rung variation. Bamboo is wonderful and sustainable, but when it breaks, it splinters in a way that stabs you. It's not going to work, and it doesn't last long enough, so I suggest we shift to pine."

"I'm sorry, what?" Ms. Cheng replied. "Why is it that you think those two ladders are the same?"

"Well, okay, for play value, the bamboo is a little lighter."

"You're thinking of the function of the ladder as a ladder, but the function of this ladder is not a ladder," Ms. Cheng said. Whoa. It was like she was uttering a Zen koan.

"When the child drops it on the floor, the bamboo sounds different than the pine does. When a child interacts with bamboo and pine ladders, they feel that there's a difference in materials. They experience a solid wood versus a hollow wood. They experience the sound. When they knock on them, they sound different. The grain feels different in their hands. They smell different."

Taking the bamboo sample in hand, she said, "Bamboo is colder, pine is warm."

I froze, my mind blown again. Now that is engaging in curious looking. Of course, this project wouldn't be as simple as I had imagined. Easy is boring. I loved the complexity of these seemingly mundane objects. But I also couldn't fathom how I was going to do the job of streamlining all these play materials when each one is so much more than a wooden block. I agreed with everything Ms. Cheng said. But we couldn't have forty types of ladders.

"Pick one," I said.

She made me figure out a way to use both.

Museums are reframing success, too. For them, that means rethinking their roles within the communities they occupy, even questioning the role of art in our lives. They are rethinking their goals. The old idea of success was measured in the number of visitors, the prestige of the permanent collection, the reputation among other institutions. Today that's changing, at least partially.

One of my most recent projects was with the Walker Art Center in Minneapolis. Initially, my design brief was to use a grant the museum received to design some fun things for children to play with as they toured the museum's collections. But then we got more ambitious. The museum was looking to find ways to make the relationship between art and viewer more porous, to go beyond adding in some playful elements to engage children during a tour. Museums should reflect the fact that a visitor—a member of the community—was there. I am not just learning from the museum; the museum is learning from me.

One element of the project at the Walker is "looking tools." When children visit the museum, they are given art supplies to make small frames of their own for looking at the art (like Sister Corita's finders). The frames can be assembled right in a gallery of the museum. Each kid gets their own with their name on it. There are tools for listening, too—repurposed ear trumpets. Kids are encouraged to touch the sculptures and to listen to them. Wooden sculptures sound different from granite, which sound different from the big hollow bronze sculptures. I tried it out. You can hear the traffic go by in the sculptures. In previous projects, I've given kids actual stethoscopes and had them listen to everything. They discover that this table sounds different from that table, just as Ms. Cheng's bamboo and pine ladders sound different.

Listening differently is possible anywhere. There are some grand churches in Europe with arched vaults that allow for a sort of game of telephone. Whispering into the stone grooves at the base of one column can be heard by someone standing at the base of the opposite one. Musicians sometimes make pieces simply by recording the ordinary sounds around them. We can make our own kind of music by tuning in to our own surroundings—whether we hear birds and water, traffic and trains, or silence. Just this morning a friend sent me an audio message of her feet crunching snow while walking to the mailbox.

There is a concept in schools called the borderless classroom, which tries to embrace the learning that happens outside the school. The same concept can apply to art, so at the Walker we pursued the idea of a "borderless museum." Because art doesn't only live in a museum. As part of that project, the kids take their frames home with them. They can keep using the looking tool as they walk down the street or ride in the car to literally reframe their everyday world. They can use it to start a conversation with their families about what they saw at the museum, and then carry on that exploration of the visual world at home. How wonderfully "successful" a museum staff can feel if they see people doing that in the galleries. It means that the visitors are fully engaged in the enterprise. Art is everywhere.

And adults can engage in reframing the world, too. We can make our own tools for looking and listening (for the latter, just close your eyes and press your ear to a window). Art—and play—is in how you see, how you look at things, what happens when you turn something upside down. It's in what you touch, taste, and smell. It's about different ways of sensing.

ADOPT A "WHAT IF" MINDSET

I think my embrace of challenge and risk is one reason that companies bring me in to talk to their employees. Sure, the Walker is an art institution, invested, by definition, in creativity (although it's just as easy for art institutions to get stodgy and stuck as any other organization). When companies are willing to accept not knowing where something is going and can stay present in the process, I can come in as an outsider and a playful human to facilitate. I'm not privy to all the rules and hierarchies that limit thinking or vision. And I don't think that much of rules or hierarchy anyway. I bring my own way of seeing, of looking at things.

Still, when Google brought me in to give a talk to their entire UX (User Experience) team—that's some five thousand people—I was a little thrown. Google wanted me to address complexity in a talk that was ultimately called "Easy is Boring." (You'll have noticed by now that's a motto of mine.) But the group I would be speaking to was made up of people whose mission is the opposite: to simplify experiences for users. I wondered, *How will my message be helpful?* It took a couple of prep meetings for me to understand how my message of complexity would be inspiring for such a team. I'll be honest. I don't want to have to click more than once to get where I want to go on a website any more than anyone else does. But I did know that even a team focused on simplifying needs to keep things fun. When easy becomes the holy grail, it's possible to forget to make things playful. When easy is everything, challenge goes out the window. Sometimes engagement happens in that challenge and people want to be engaged. When we figure things out, they feel like our own.

In cases like the Google talk, I'm a provocateur, a person with a "what if . . ." mindset. An exercise from my design classes captures this idea exactly. For the first twenty minutes of every class (these are six-hour studio classes), we engage in a "play sprint." These can be a newly designed activity or a variation on a classic—something to "hack." The constraints are that the game must be something we can do in twenty minutes and cannot call for materials beyond paper. We playtest the activity as a group. Maybe it's a Rochambeau (paper, scissors, rock) tournament. As we play, we ask "What if?" to redesign on the fly. We play it again. What if you are allowed to invent new tools on the fly? What if three people play at once? Play. Discuss. Replay.

Several things happen. First, it's fun. We could spend hours on these play sprints instead of twenty minutes. Second, ownership shifts to the whole group. Students propose a game for us all knowing the concept will become something else entirely through trial and error. The whole point is to collaboratively change it. Success in a play sprint lies wholly in the process, in the experience, and has nothing to do with the outcome, with who wins, or if the game "works."

That's what I mean by being a play provocateur. Companies benefit from hearing from someone who has a totally different approach to the problems they confront every day. Success for Google's UX shouldn't always be defined—or only be defined—as using as few clicks as possible. Success could be that people enjoyed using whatever was created, even if they had to work a little harder to do it. Success could also mean asking "What if?" about sacred cows. The ever-changing Google logo on the landing page is a good example. Most companies don't change their logo. Ever. But the Google doodles are fun and keep you guessing on what is otherwise a wonderfully simple page.

Being a play provocateur in our own lives means challenging ourselves, asking "What if?" all the time and creating nonlinear paths with the materials of our day-to-day existence. It means seeking out the difference between bamboo and pine. It means asking ourselves what we were curious about. It means looking at risk as a positive, and metaphorically finding our own "courage log." It means embracing failure as the way to find the things that don't work. And it means recognizing that play can be as important as anything else and perhaps reordering our priorities. Who decides *that* is more important than *this*? We can take agency in our own lives and declare our own hierarchy of importance.

When we do that, I imagine us strolling through the world like the Anji Play kids, recognizing the tools of our play—the ladders and barrels and sandbags, so to speak—in the wider world and telling ourselves, *Hey, I know what that is*, and *I know how to use it*. And when we imagine using it, it might well be in ways the maker hadn't intended. Great! We will be up for the challenge.

8

BE YOUR OWN PLAYWORKER

Not to brag, but most people under the age of twelve think that my life rules. Maybe we have similar priorities. Maybe it's a tendency toward extremes. Either way, for years I lived in what could easily be described as a kid fantasy.

Camp Fun was a ramshackle set of buildings on five acres that had once been a campground and then a summer camp for kids. I bought the property and moved in after my first year of teaching at RISD. I was excited to use the barn as my woodshop and the meadow on the property to prototype full-scale playthings. I set about building my primary residence and cultivating a place where friends and chosen family could gather. To lure friends up from NYC (a four-hour train ride), it had to be epic. There was no television, and cellular service and the internet were patchy on a good day. There was a nearly full-length basketball court, a swimming pool with a rickety slide from 1978, an outdoor shower, and the biggest trampoline I could find for free on Craigslist (14 feet in diameter). There was a pond teeming with crawdads and frogs, paths through the woods, fruit trees, and endless projects. Adult Summer Camp.

Over the course of the ten years that I lived there, we held three weddings and at least three children were conceived. There were specific weekends and occasions throughout the year when people would descend upon the property, supplies in hand, and leave days later exhausted, inspired, grounded. I hesitate to say I hosted parties, since I was less of a host and more of a provocateur. And they were not so much parties as emergent collaborative play dates. To say my hosting style is unstructured is an understatement. I designed Camp Fun the way I design everything, creating the conditions for free play to arise. How could I know what kind of play my friends needed on any given day? The environment afforded finding what you needed, and inevitably they did.

But my first season there was rough. I'd moved in the middle of January with my friend Jeff who helped me fix it up in exchange for rent. The main house was partially on the grid, but still had a hand-dug well and a cesspool, which I hesitate to admit were a little too close to each other. The boiler was moody, and the outdoor oil tank kept freezing. I love a project, but the scale of this place was daunting. For the first year, the friends who came up from NYC for the weekend were the ones for whom projects are play.

Colleen was one of the guests. She and I have been friends since 1998, when she worked at the dyke bar that my then-girlfriend owned. Colleen showed up at the Lexington Club at the age of seventeen and demanded a job.

"You can't even come inside. How can you work here!?" was the obvious response.

"I'll work door."

Her gall became her primary qualification, and she was somehow hired. Unrelated to her irreverence for rules, she's great at math, so she and I set about one weekend to replace a drafty door. I had planned for most of what we needed, and her diligence—measure twice, cut once—made up for my bad math. After a hard day's work, we went outside to cook on a fire. This is my go-to. If there can be a fire, I will make food on it. But midway through cooking, it started to rain. We grabbed the grill with all the vegetables on it and ran toward the house. "The fireplace?" I hesitated. It made sense—we could build a very similar fire to put this grill over, but it seemed strange or wrong to cook on a fire indoors. My Adult Voice had opinions. *The stove is right there! You'll get food juice in the fireplace!* We stood in the entryway, haphazardly holding the hot grill with fire tongs, debating our next move. We kept finding reasons not to grill in the fireplace, but all of them were adult reasons. We likely heard them or some related logic from our parents, and sure, kids probably shouldn't just cook food in the fireplace every time they need a snack. But we were adults, and this was my house, which I owned. I got to make my own rules about how to use it, my own version of adulthood, one that prioritized play.

I deferred to my Play Voice, and we rearranged the furniture to get two lounge chairs directly in front of the fireplace and finished cooking our dinner. Naturally this was followed by roasting marshmallows in the fireplace, which we suspected and confirmed carried a high risk of sticky mess. The whole thing was a playtest. We didn't know how it would go but we were curious and excited to try. With the help of the dogs, we cleaned up the marshmallow phase and settled into Colleen's music playlist. This, for me, usually cues the last stage of the nightly outdoor bonfire: whittling. I took out my pocketknife and considered the consequences of bringing another outside activity inside, which really amounted to wood shavings on the floor.

"Colleen, I'm gonna do it," I announced.

She sighed. "Now's the time," she said, pointing over her shoulder to the Shop-Vac sitting ready next to our door project.

"No, I mean always. Let's always whittle indoors. This will be that kind of house! Play overrules civility or whatever logic usually wins and makes us not carve wood inside!"

Thus began the unraveling of all my adult logic. From then on, I determined to prioritize play in everything about Camp Fun and my life there. I would listen to my Play Voice.

And I did. Every Fourth of July, fifteen to twenty people would come stay for a few days. Everybody arrived bearing food and playthings ranging from cheap pool toys to costumes to laser light shows that we installed in the woods. We embraced openended. People cooked and ate together, but nothing was explicitly planned or organized. The conditions inspired people to grab what they needed and do what they wanted. As social creatures we tended to orbit one activity at a time. For example, the readers would read next to the pool or the trampoline depending on where the group was playing. But there were always a solitary few guests chopping wood or drawing near the brook. I kept a guitar on hand and would place it somewhere obvious in the hopes it would inspire music. It often did, but I'd never force it.

There were also moments of stillness and solitude. The brook made several turns and broad curves before reaching the pond, and each formed an area with a distinct mood. One had a shady carpet of moss and smelled incredible. Conversation there tended toward hushed and intimate. Another had boulders and sunshine and looked onto the trampoline, where all kinds of play erupted. Hanging out there, people forgot about the outside world. It was safe and contained yet expansive, as the best playgrounds are.

Like a playworker at an adventure playground, I would introduce things without knowing where they would go or what we could do with them and then watch how the group integrated them into the weekend's activities. I wasn't telling anyone what to do. I was offering possibilities. Everybody would be at the pool doing their thing and I would think, *Wouldn't it be cool if . . .* or *What would the group do with . . . What if I brought out . . .* I would go get a Super Soaker for the slide or make a new inflatable by attaching the head from the blow-up swan to a floating crocodile. Or I would bring out sparklers or glue. I always took it up a notch.

Guests didn't always need my prompts. Everybody participated in just about everything that happened. Just as free play for kids is child-directed, the weekend's activities were friend-directed. For some guests, things that would normally be considered work became play because they were outside of their everyday lives. One friend spent half a day chopping wood every time he visited. There's something about being removed from habits that allows for a different kind of fun. And it's easier for chores to become play when they aren't your own.

But it is possible to make chores feel like play even when they are essential to daily living. And it is possible to do that at home, to put a little Camp Fun into everyday life. I'll be the first to acknowledge that a swimming pool and room for twenty people to stay—however ramshackle the accommodations—are luxuries. Fortunately, you don't need those things in order to play. There wasn't anything magical that happened when people crossed my property line. What happened was that visitors embraced the spirit of the place. Camp Fun was geared to play, but mainly it represented a mindset. When they got there, my guests adopted the perspective that whatever they were doing there (even work) could be fun, that they didn't have to take themselves too seriously. Adult Voices weren't in charge. Play Voices ruled the place.

We can make our lives more like Camp Fun in all kinds of ways—subtle and not so subtle—if we give ourselves permission, if we see the playful possibilities that surround us and live in us. "This is the real secret of life—to be completely engaged with what you are doing in the here and now," said the author and speaker Alan Watts. "And instead of calling it work, realize it is play."

We can do that by engaging in the kind of play that I've been calling for throughout this book, free play that embraces possibility, releases judgment, and reframes success. When we do, it is intoxicating. The playwright S. N. Behrman captured the feeling beautifully when he described being in the room when his friend George Gershwin sat down at the piano to play for his friends just for the fun of it. You "felt on the instant the newness, the humor, above all the great heady surf of vitality. The room became freshly oxygenated; everybody felt it, everybody breathed it."

Fresh oxygen—that's what play is. It breathes new life into us.

EVERYWHERE YOU LOOK

Opportunities for play are everywhere. In nature, on city sidewalks, in our daily errands, at work. One reason we don't recognize them is that we tend to compartmentalize behaviors and activities in ways that aren't helpful: We exercise at the gym, relax at yoga, connect with partners over dinner. By integrating play throughout the day, we desegregate our lives. Play can happen on our commute to work as much as at a dinner party. It can happen at the office in the way we interact with colleagues or the way we brainstorm. It can happen in the way we approach our chores. I know of an architect who illustrated the weekly grocery list. For me, the hardware store is the candy store. I go to my local Ace to get something very specific and leave with 20 pounds of metal joints I can't wait to play with. Bookstores can be that way, too—enticing invitations to lose yourself for a time or find yourself in a new way.

Something I like about social media is the way it showcases people being playful. From "here's this funny thing my friend did for me" to elaborately staged videos, we glance into each other's homes or collaboratively riff on a theme. In the original form of the game Exquisite Corpse, for example, each player takes turns writing or drawing on a sheet of paper and folds it to conceal their contribution and pass it along. Now there's a digitally enabled version, which features the varied creativity and skills of millions of collaborators.

Look for chances to play with your own children (or other people's children, of course). When adults play with kids, it's often parallel play—people are playing the same thing at the same time, but not necessarily together. If you've ever colored or drawn with a child, or played with blocks, this was likely parallel play. It's also a great opening for you to do your own things with whatever materials are being used. Permission is there. You've already created a nonjudgmental space and given attention to play, so embrace curiosity and see what happens. A word of warning: Kids might be surprised. I've experienced kids being caught off guard when I'm playing as enthusiastically as they are. It breaks a rule that they've come to understand about adults. They expect us to support their play. They tell us, "Watch this" and "Do that." They don't always know what to do with an adult who wants to be in the play equally. We can remind those children—and ourselves—that we were all born knowing how to play.

Sometimes whole cities or even whole countries play together. Songkran is a water festival held every spring in Thailand. The idea is to mark moving forward. Water is featured symbolically to wash away the previous year. In addition to gentle traditions like young people pouring water on the hands of elderly relatives, people take to the streets for what amounts to a nationwide water fight. People come armed with buckets, squirt guns, and any other containers they can think of to throw water at friends and splash the crowds. Something similar happens in India during Holi, a festival of color when people throw colored water and powders at each other and generally make merry together. La Tomatina takes place in August in Spain. It's known as the biggest food fight in the world and as the name suggests, people throw tomatoes at each other, with glee. Closer to home there's Gay Pride and the parades and street fairs that take up much of the month of June. But the gay community doesn't limit celebratory behavior to that one time of year. Like Emma Goldman who rejected the idea of a revolution that didn't allow dancing, we dance everywhere and all the time. Play is collective rebellion as well as celebration.

If the idea of joining a jostling crowd is anathema to you, remember all the times you stopped to appreciate a rainbow or a spectacular sunset or the drama of a gathering storm. Those were moments of attention play. When a large swath of the United States came to a brief stop and gazed skyward for the total eclipse in April of 2024, that, too, was attention play, a shared version that was spiritual and awe-inspiring for many of us.

Recognize the play types you might already be engaging in. Puzzles on a rainy day are meditative play. Storytelling at bedtime is creative play. Getting jostled at a concert is embodied play. In fact, much of what I learned about this form of play I learned at riot grrrl shows, by trusting in the motion of a crowd. New Year's Eve in Times Square is the same. And what about the running of the bulls in Pamplona, Spain? That is about as embodied as it gets.

Singing encompasses multiple play types depending on how

we do it. Singing at the top of your lungs in the car or the shower? Creative play, embodied play, and a little possibility play if you throw in a drum solo on the dashboard or the bathroom wall. When we sing with other people, it serves as a connector. When we sing solo, we entertain ourselves, and maybe explore identities. It becomes what we need it to be depending on the situation.

It's not a big leap from singing at the top of your lungs to yelling at a game or a wonderful performance. That isn't just a way of rooting on the athletes or performers; it's a pressure release valve. It's physical. I often notice that when I go to WNBA games here in Brooklyn, where the New York Liberty play. There's a moment where we're all yelling, just for the fun of it. We gladly . . . Make . . . Some . . . Noise as the Jumbotron instructs.

Anything that can't be deemed a productive use of time can be (mis)behavior play and incredibly fulfilling, exactly what you needed, whether it's taking the long route home, tinkering with your bicycle, or putting on elaborate makeup only to wash it off before bed.

When's the last time you gazed out a window? I travel a lot for work and at some point, without noticing, I shifted from choosing a window seat to choosing an aisle on the left side of the plane, specifically so that my right elbow would be uninhibited to sketch (i.e., work) during the flight. Periodically, I'd notice the person in the window glued to the view, gazing out at the land below or the expanse of clouds and sky. For me, choosing the aisle seat was a stubbornly adult phase in which I thought myself beyond the magic and mystery of gazing out the window. The aisle seat has power—and the pretense that one is above such childlike amazement. My Adult Voice is unimpressed by the feat of imagination and engineering that gets us up into the sky at all. But my Play Voice wants to gaze! It wants to imagine the lives below, to follow the winding roads, the quilted patchwork of industrial zones and farmland, the twisting grids of suburban sprawl, the ribbons of white that light up the earth at night. When I am bounding along atop the fluffy white and gray splendor of clouds, I appreciate the seemingly endless variation and I half expect a Hanna-Barbera Flying Machine or a creation from a Miyazaki film to float by. I'm back to window seats now.

Outdoors at night, how can we not be afraid of the dark? By engaging in attention play. The bubble of light made by a flashlight feels protective. Everything outside, in the dark, becomes unknown and dangerous. It's "other." Pointing the flashlight doesn't illuminate the sounds you hear. The noises of the dark don't care about your light bubble. Years of seeds planted by horror movies begin to sprout and you imagine danger lurking in every shadow. If your light bubble doesn't protect you, what if you don't create the bubble in the first place? What if you leave the light off and let yourself be part of the dark, part of the woods, part of the shadows, just another creature moving in the dark, attuned to the movements of other creatures around you, things too small to see. You are now part of the thing that was scary when you were separated from it. I guarantee you'll walk differently. Your feet feel for variations in the path. Your other senses help out, and there is more information to identify your surroundings. Darkness isn't something to fix with the flash of your smartphone; it's something to experience, be curious about. A light would help you get from the bonfire to the bathroom much faster, but where's the play in that?

We can approach sex with a similar curiosity. One colleague said she and her partner recently had a pillow fight that became a sort of foreplay, which in turn made the sex different. She was surprised by this unexpected outcome. I asked how it was different. She thought for a moment then smiled and said, "We giggled more, the vibe was light, easy."

In sex we can experience risk, vulnerability, and connection all while engaging our senses, mind, and body—all elements of play. I say "We *can* experience . . ." because of course all those elements are not always part of sex. A willingness to be vulnerable seems to me to be a primary factor in how playful the sex is. There is a vulnerability in being naked (or some variation thereof). Exposing yourself, literally and figuratively, is not a thing most of us do regularly or easily. As with many ways of playing, the dynamic between players inspires us to venture into other parts of ourselves. Perhaps we're attuned to our partner and responding to the nuance of their energy, or maybe the uncertainty of a casual encounter adds tension and thrill. Either way, there is excitement in what might arise from communicating with your body, responding to touch, experiencing the intensity of attention to multiple senses. That collective flow state is play.

BRAVELY YOU

Each of us has a propensity toward some types of play more than others. Who will meet for a spontaneous picnic on a beautiful day? Who's willing to jump on a bike and see where it takes you? And who prefers to schedule a couple weeks out—those glorious humans who read the reviews and buy tickets and seem to have secret information about the city just by virtue of actually making plans? Anyone who buys tickets needs someone to go with them. Be a playful friend. Say yes.

Occasionally we find ourselves confronted with each other's approaches in ways that help us understand even those we think we know. During another time when Colleen was visiting Camp Fun, we found ourselves with a brand-new boxed LEGO set— the Volkswagen camper van—a gift from the Danish team I'd been working with for a LEGO-sponsored class I was teaching at RISD. Without hesitation we dove in, and an hour in we were contentedly working away, drinking wine, telling stories, catching up. Until I noticed she'd stopped building. The van seemed to be coming along, although I hadn't looked at the instructions once. I'd just been grabbing pieces and making whatever came to mind as I put them together. "What's up?" I asked, looking at her for the first time since we began. She paused, let out a stiff sigh, and only then did I notice the clench in her jaw. "What the fuck are you doing?" she asked me with what can only be described as patient contempt. I then surveyed the coffee table and saw her carefully separated piles of bricks, organized by . . . color? or size? No, it was something else. I looked more closely, trying to decipher her logic. . . . What mysterious code was Colleen playing by? I looked from the piles to the in-progress camper van to her tense face and only then saw, in the center of the table, the key element that I'd been acutely unaware of until then. The instructions. How had I forgotten about the instructions?

"Oh. Crap. I'm sorry; are you actually following those?"

"*Yes*, I'm following them. We're making the van! But you keep taking random pieces we need so we're not actually getting anywhere!"

Well, I thought, *I'm getting somewhere, it's just not the same place you thought we were going.* But I didn't share that thought. Instead, I tried to understand.

"It's fun for you to assemble the thing even though they're telling you how?"

She laughed, amazed that I'd even ask. "*Dude*, yes!"

Colleen, this human I loved and one of my closest friends, was playing in the exact way that all my work was trying to counterbalance. And she seemed to be really enjoying it. So, I took apart my unremarkable work-in-progress and turned my attention to the instructions. We continued laughing, playing music, and tracking which page and parts we were on, having a great evening doing what felt to me like a puzzle rather than a creative building time. But the goal was to hang out, and I got not only that but to play in a way that was new to me and very natural to my pal. The VW camper van in its assembled state lasted about a week at Camp Fun. A friend came by with her kids, so I put it out where they'd see it. They immediately destroyed (aka deconstructed) it and made a bunch of other things, nothing specific, nothing remarkable, all of it exactly what it needed to be in their play.

PLAY PROMPTS

Throughout the book, I've proposed some tools you can use—with your friends or alone—to inspire your own play. You can use your past to inspire your present by tapping into your play memories. You can find things in your life today that cry out for playtesting. You can create your own constraints, think sideways, and curiously engage with whatever lies in front of you. You could also get in the habit of visualizing your future play by practicing play projecting. We do this for our work by aspiring to promotions and imagining success. We do this with our relationships when we fantasize about moving in with someone. Why not imagine what a more playful life would look like, too?

Remember that my version of adult free play is rooted in the definition of free play for children, what Penny Wilson described as "freely chosen, personally directed, and intrinsically motivated." What that means will be different for each of us. For me this translates to a fair bit of dillydally, some frivolity, and lots of tinkering. For my sister, Tisha, it still looks like losing herself in a book for hours.

I am offering possibilities. And I am reminding you that play is something you can't be good or bad at. It grows out of our personalities and our accumulated childhood experiences—the things we loved and the things we hated, the things we lost and the things we found. Play is essential to maturity, Lenore Terr wrote. "Play is a lost key. It unlocks the door to ourselves."

Since free play for adults has less to do with the activities we engage in than with our mindset, we need to find ways to shift perspective. Many of the ideas and techniques I use in my work can help hone a playful approach to everyday life. They remind us to see the world with curiosity, to not worry so much about being taken seriously, and to remember that success comes in many shapes and sizes. The goal is to be the one extending the world a hand to dance, or happily accepting one when it is offered.

DIARY OF A DEJECTED PLAYVOICE

The dog you didn't play with

Here are some actual prompts, some borrowed, some variations on classics from childhood that still resonate:

Wear something that feels out of character and notice how it changes the way you interact with the world and the way people interact with you.

Next time you're sitting near a quiet brook, consider rearranging some rocks to make it babble.

Practice curiosity on your next hike, peek under a log now and then.

When friends come over, have everyone sit on the floor and see how it changes the conversation.

Converse in song. Replace lyrics to a known tune, à la "Weird Al" Yankovic.

Translate for animals. What are those birds going on about? That squirrel has a lot of opinions. I love doing this when I'm walking my dog. Encounters with other dogs are rich and filled with inaudible dialogue.

Break a habit. Sleep on the other side of the bed or with your feet at the head. Take a shower with the lights off. Brush your teeth with the opposite hand.

Make the fart joke. My family reveled in them. "There goes a mouse on a motorcycle," my stepdad would say. Or "Who kicked a duck?"

Go on mundane adventures. There are discoveries to be made at the grocery store, artifacts to collect, villains to avoid. Make your companion your co-conspirator.

Clues are everywhere. Notice what's around you—anything from litter to an out-of-place tree—and invent a story about how it got there. As I walk around the city, I'll often intertwine what I see into one ongoing mystery.

LET YOUR PLAY EVOLVE

A playful perspective helps us stay flexible. Ten years into owning Camp Fun, something began to shift in what I needed. As much as I loved the immersive weekends with friends there, I missed the impromptu gatherings that happen in the city. My work required I spend more time in New York City, and I found myself drawn to its energy and social ease. Living at Camp Fun was becoming less . . . fun.

People were surprised, especially my eight-year-old friend Hue. If you ever want to get an eight-year-old in a contemplative mood, find a high spot, such as a cliff, or a big rock, or a tree, and climb there with them. Once you get there, just sit quietly and see what comes up. For Hue and me, this happened on the roof of a cabin at Camp Fun.

The cabin was built into a slope that led to a pond. That meant one side of the roof was only five feet off the ground while the other side overlooked the pond and the dense woods beyond. Hue had been coming to Camp Fun since he was around three. He learned how to get on the roof from the older kids who perfected a system of access over the course of each summer. One year they used a ladder that had rusted and was stuck open where I had been pruning a peach tree near the slope. They'd drag it over to the low side of the roof and clamber up, staying up there for hours. Another year, a teenager got involved and tied a rope around the chimney so they all could pull themselves up. This led to more acrobatics than roof time (and was ultimately deemed too rough on the shingles). Another season the kids found a pallet next to the firewood pile. They leaned the pallet against an upturned log, which got them just close enough to hoist the tallest kid onto the roof. That kid would then give a hand to all the others. This was a great system until someone wanted down, at which point they'd yell for adult backup. I loved that they'd try every possible solution before asking us for help.

I didn't join the crew on the roof until the last year I owned the place. That was the year a warbler nested in one of the nooks of the hut's stone chimney. When the kids spotted the eggs, they called to me from the roof to see whether I knew when they'd hatch. I took it as an invitation to join them on their perch. Until then I had been busy playing with the adults, respecting the roof as the kids' turf, like a tree house with a handmade No Grown-Ups sign.

Pleased to be asked, I ascended to check on the eggs even though I have no idea how to read a nest, or eggs, or birds, for that matter. Once I was up there and declared the eggs healthy, I settled in with the kids to watch the rest of the party beneath us. A couple kids left to help gather kindling and start a fire. Another few left to have one last jump in the pool before it got too cold. Eventually it was just Hue and me.

"You aren't really going to move from Camp Fun, are you?" he asked.

"I am . . ." is as far as I got before I realized I didn't know how to answer him. Should I explain that maintaining Camp Fun was distracting me from other work? That yes, of course, I'd rather repair the bridge than answer emails, that both of those things needed to happen, but only one pays my bills. If I said it was lonely to live there, Hue would look at me like my hair was on fire. Every time he's visited, Camp Fun was a giant glorious frolicking party. But when everyone left, there was just me.

Adult priorities are confusing. Moving from Camp Fun to a tiny apartment in Brooklyn was never going to make sense to Hue. It didn't even consistently make sense to me, but I was doing it.

"I am . . ." I repeated.

We sat in silence as I faced my own conflicted interests. The light was changing. Partygoers were migrating toward the kitchen. Parents began searching for long-abandoned shoes. I noticed my dogs anxiously looking for me. As smoke from the bonfire began to waft toward us, we stood up and brushed bits of shingles from our shorts.

I paused and said to Hue, and myself, "It's time for a new adventure."

And when I said it, I knew that was the answer. Camp Fun had been wonderful. It had served its purpose. I had created a place where my Play Voice—and everyone else's—held sway.

I bought the place to prioritize play.

And now I was selling the place to prioritize play.

Both things can be true. What we need to support play in our lives can—and will—shift over time. The trick is staying current with our own desires. It took me time to see that. But I knew I had embraced the possibilities of the place. It had been a beautifully judgment-free zone, where all play was welcome. Now I was releasing judgment about selling it and reframing success. I didn't have to keep Camp Fun to keep playing.

I felt the siren call of another sort of play. I'd been out of New York City for thirteen years. As much as I love playing in nature, I also love playing with other people. I missed New York City and its museums, clubs, and parks.

I moved back to Brooklyn and my overlook shifted from the roof of a cabin to an apartment terrace. I sit and drink my coffee there every morning, watching my neighborhood unfold beneath me like in *Richard Scarry's Busy, Busy Town*. People bustle in and out of the subway entrance. A dogwalker rassles dogs into a joyous pack and steers around the line for the coffee shop. The barber smokes a cigarette on the sidewalk and heckles the teens gathered on a park bench who leap into one another's TikTok videos. The garbage collectors fling bags into the trucks before the rats can get to them. A jogger runs past the small grocer on the corner where they know me by name. Next door, pigeons from a rooftop cote swoop in formation, then settle in front of the tailor's storefront where he leaves them crumbs. In true Brooklyn form, the people are all shapes, sizes, and ethnicities. I imagine where they're headed, who they're thinking about hurrying to meet, what's going on in their lives.

I redesigned my life so that (new) conditions for play could arise.

FIND WHAT YOU NEED

The week before the 2024 presidential election, I did a workshop with a group of design professionals. I was distracted and could tell my colleagues were, too. Before my session, I overheard conversations about people feeling helpless, burned out, sad. They were struggling to stay connected to their kids and partners. They were having difficulty getting work done or sleeping well. Nationwide, we were reeling.

Right before the workshop started, someone leaned over and said to me, "I don't envy you, Cas, this is a heavy mood. How on earth are you going to get us to play?" But honestly, this is exactly when we need to play.

I'm always aware of context in my work and teaching, responsive to the people in the room and the goings-on around them. We don't operate in a vacuum. I leaned into the distraction and unease in the room, introducing myself with full transparency.

"I have no idea what I need right now, let alone how to get it," I said. "Whatever tools help us manage anxiety are probably maxed out or ill-suited to this prolonged period of uncertainty and fear. Maybe the act of looking for what you need, of trying to identify it, is enough. When we explore what we need in the context of play, we don't necessarily expect to get it. Sometimes, we do. Sometimes, we don't. But the act of trying, the gesture of attention and effort, gives us some agency."

I had brought a variety of props ranging from wooden blocks and dice to foam yoga rollers and spiky massage balls. I put them out on the floor and arranged people in groups of three. Then I prompted them. "Design a playful way to get what you need. Take a familiar game from childhood and redesign it. We'll play-test each game. You have sixteen minutes. Go."

I'm aware that "What do you need?" is an incomplete question. What do I need to do what? To feel okay? To function? To sleep at night? To be present with my kids? To have conversations with my neighbors and loved ones whose views and values differ drastically from mine? This would be a hang-up in a normal design brief. To solve a problem, you begin by defining it.

But play isn't problem-solving.

We weren't trying to make this need go away. The goal wasn't to fix anyone.

Get what you need.

As they got started, I bounced from group to group. I re-minded them to brainstorm by doing, to demonstrate their ideas by playing. I overheard memories of recess games as well as very personal explorations of what everyone needed.

With three minutes left, I asked them to name their game and prepare to instruct others how to play. I noticed they were appropriating things that were already in the room. A few bean-bags had turned into "castles." A stanchion rope came off the wall and onto the floor.

When it was time to share, they introduced their games. The first was called Bumbling Ducky. Three players faced one another inside the stanchion rope "pond." The goal was to lift the pond up to their necks without using their hands, which were occupied holding random objects—a stack of books, two rubber balls, and finger puppets. To do this seemingly useless task, the players had to contort their bodies into all sorts of odd shapes. Shoulders wound up next to knees as they twisted to prevent the rope from sliding off their partners. They looked absurd. The room erupted in cheers when the chunky velvet pond finally rested on everyone's shoulders.

What did they need? Apparently, to move their bodies in silly ways. To be in tune with two other people. To complete a futile and seemingly pointless task. To play.

In another game, the winner got to scream. I don't think any of us have been so competitive in years. We *needed* to scream.

A third group designed Hide and Sleep. They had only to say the name and everyone took heed, immediately darting in all directions, ducking under tables, tucking themselves into corners. A quiet hush came over the room, and I noticed that we'd found and made forts not just for ourselves but for pairs or small groups. People lay under tables in piles of coats, their feet resting on chairs or poking out between overturned tables. Most were talking in calm, intimate tones. There was giggling. It was social, meditative play.

What did they need? To rest, even if only to acknowledge that by seeking it. To hide, that was unmistakable. To change perspective. To connect to a peer in a new way. Lying on the floor, in protected, small spaces allowed talk about things they might not have gotten to in a different posture. It created the conditions for intimacy.

A participant who worked in the building and walked past this spot every day said she had never thought to climb underneath the counter. She recognized the moment when her perspective shifted. "There's something about following curiosity," she said. "You invited us to wonder what it would feel like to go under there or lie like this. Something shifted and I was feeling instead of thinking." She paused, and the room waited while she found the words. "I feel fulfilled."

What do you need? Let play be a tool that will help you figure this out. There is no right answer.

It may seem that I've stumbled on an inherent contradiction. This is a book meant to help you (re)learn how to play, yet I've extolled the virtues of play without instructions. Instead of instructions, I've given you permission. To play, yes, but also to embrace possibility, release judgment, reframe success.

I'm an inventor and design things for people to play with. This book is no exception. Like all my creations, it will not be complete until you make it your own. Find ideas that inspire, ideas to integrate, ideas to playtest. Reconnect with your playful mindset and unlearn how to *not* play. Trust yourself and your Play Voice and be your own playworker.

Set up your life to create the conditions for play to arise.

ACKNOWLEDGMENTS

Cas Holman

It's an impossible task to acknowledge all who've influenced, inspired, and contributed to the work that informed this book. I do my best to express gratitude along the way and show up for people the way so many have shown up for me. That said, a few have made a direct impact on making this real.

I am thankful (and lucky) that Kirby Kim saw an idea worth exploring and continued to believe in it through a few rounds of funky iterations. This book would have taken ten years instead of five if not for the talents of Lydia Denworth, who was a curious translator and organizer of these ideas. I'm grateful to Lucia Watson for trusting me, Isabel McCarthy for her patient persistence, and Jess Morphew for being great. I couldn't do much of anything without my brave, steady team: Amanda Gates-Elston, Jane Chudinov, Bridget Keller, Doug Johnson, and Amy Rodrigues—all of whom have helped build something wonderful.

I'm eternally grateful to Scott Dadich, Chai Vasarhelyi, Paula Chowles, Clair Popkin, and Bari Pearlman of *Abstract: The Art of Design* for telling my story with boldness and joy. And to Julia Reagan Dubray for what's to come next. Thank you to Marc Hacker and David Rockwell, who early on let my work be play, and Barry Richards, who reminded me to put holes in everything. Thanks to John Maeda for giving me confidence in the intelligence of weird.

Thanks to Cheng Xueqin, Jesse Coffino, Chelsea Bailey, and Anji Play Schools for showing me that ideal is possible and will be formed by children through play. I've never felt as much hope as I did during the time spent in those schools. To Mary Cunningham, Ngina Johnson, and many other kindergarten teachers who've taught me how to learn from children and encouraged me to be brave in designing for them.

I'm grateful for all the playmates who lent their curious minds and talents to playtesting ideas in this book: Karen Hewitt, Carly Ciarrocchi, Garrett Jaeger, Andrew Sliwinski, Tovah Klein, Jocelyn Davis, Colleen Arnerich, Milo Wippermann, Shira Klein, Tucker Viemeister, Eri Nagasaka, and Shoham Arad. And to Samantha Seneviratne for deeply important giggling, Alex White for witchcraft and hand-holding, and Mox Raleigh Trissel for critical reads and powerful love.

Thanks to Mom and Tisha for living room dance parties, camping in the wild, and jumping from high rocks into cold rivers. Dad for teaching me how to talk to ghosts, listen to my guardian angel, and read plants. Thanks to Howard and Heidi Snell—my favorite aunt and uncle, whose intuitive joy in exploring unseen versions of adulthood showed me I could shape my own. To Paolo, Valeria, Petra, and Nora for adopting me into their family as uncle, sibling, bonus spouse, and freeloader.

I wouldn't be who I am today without Steven Thor Grygelko (Heklina) and TShack. A community who loved and embraced me as a joyful, feisty little brother. I've never felt so seen or inspired to play. And to Sergio Prieto, Lila Thirkield, Maria Carapetti, and Sahar Khoury, with whom I laid a foundation of adulthood that let me grow into something true.

Lydia Denworth

I'm so grateful to Cas Holman for bringing me along on the *Playful* journey. From the moment I was introduced to her work in the *Abstract* documentary, I was hooked. Working together has been a joy, and oh so playful! There were dogs, slides, LEGOs, and Rigamajig, plus hours and hours of excellent conversation. I have taken her ideas to heart and brought more play back into my own life. I'm here to say that playtesting life really does work. Thank you, Cas, for all of it.

Thanks to Kirby Kim for thinking of me for this project, and to Lucia Watson and Isabel McCarthy at Avery for the opportunity, for laughing at the right spots and pushing when we needed pushing. And as always, a sincere thanks to my agent, Dorian Karchmar, whose wisdom and support are invaluable. I know how lucky I am.

Thanks to my friends and family, who are willing to play early and often. Special thanks to Moira Bailey, for being the very best sounding board and making me laugh every time we speak, and to my accountability team, especially Christine Kenneally, for cheering me on. Thanks to Jacob, Matthew, and Alex for reminding me what matters—in play and otherwise. And finally, thanks to Mark, with whom I've found a new spirit of play.

DIARY OF A DEJECTED PLAYVOICE

The cracks you stepped on, ignoring pleas not to break your mother's back.

NOTES

1: THE CONDITIONS FOR PLAY

7   **In a study of architects:** Donald W. MacKinnon, "The Nature and Nurture of Creative Talent," *American Psychologist* 17, no. 7 (1962): 484–95.

7   **at Cal Tech's Jet Propulsion Laboratory:** Stuart Brown, *Play: How It Shapes the Brain, Opens the Imagination, and Invigorates the Soul* (Avery, 2010), 9–11.

9   **"Trying to define play":** Quoted in Penny Wilson, *The Playwork Primer* (Alliance for Childhood, 2010), 5.

9   **The following are:** Bob Hughes, *Play Types: Speculations and Possibilities* (The London Centre for Playwork, Education and Training, 2006).

9   **Penny Wilson, one of the leaders:** Wilson, *The Playwork Primer*, 5.

12   **"You can teach creativity":** John Cleese, *Creativity: A Short and Cheerful Guide* (Crown, 2020), 5–6.

17   **by our midtwenties:** Jay N. Giedd, "The Amazing Teen Brain," *Scientific American*, May 2016.

2: PLAY IS IN US

25   **These tracks:** Matthew R. Bennett et al., "Exceptional Preservation of Children's Footprints from a Holocene Footprint Site in Namibia," *Journal of African Earth Sciences* 97 (2014): 331–41.

26   **they were being "playful":** Matthew Bennett, "What Ancient Footprints Can Tell Us About What It Was Like to Be a Child in Prehistoric Times," *The Conversation*, February 12, 2018.

31   **Play is critical:** Sandra Aamodt and Sam Wang, *Welcome to Your Child's Brain: From in Utero to Uni* (ONEWorld Publications, 2011), chap. 14, "Playing for Keeps."

31   **Psychoanalyst Erik Erikson:** Cited in Charles E. Schaefer, "Play Therapy" in G. Pirooz Sholevar et al., eds, *Emotional Disorders in Children and Adolescents*, Child Behavior and Development (Springer, 1980): 95–105.

31   **Play is so essential:** United Nations, Human Rights, Office of the High Commissioner, Convention on the Rights of the Child, adopted November 20, 1989, Article 31.

32   **"The adult . . . often seems":** Erikson quoted in Lenore Terr, *Beyond Love and Work: Why Adults Need to Play* (Simon & Schuster, 1999), 13.

32   **"For many years":** Johan Huizinga, foreword to *Homo Ludens: A Study of the Play-Element in Culture* (Beacon Press, 1955).

32   **"We might call it":** Huizinga, *Homo Ludens*, 13.

32   **idea of "flow":** Mihaly Csikszentmihalyi, *Flow: The Psychology of Optimal Experience* (Harper Perennial Modern Classics, 1990), 4, Kindle.

33   **Anthropologists who followed:** Phillips Stevens Jr., "Yes, We Need a Neuroscience of Play," *International Journal of Play* 9, no. 1 (2020): 160–69.

33   **Play, we know now:** For example, Marian C. Diamond et al., "The Effects of an Enriched Environment on the Histology of the Rat Cerebral Cortex," *Journal of Comparative Neurology* 123, no. 1

(1964): 111–19. Also described in Stuart Brown, *Play: How it Shapes the Brain, Opens the Imagination, and Invigorates the Soul* (Avery, 2010), 38–40.

34   **From the moment babies:** See Center on the Developing Child, Harvard University, "Key Concepts: Brain Architecture," https://developingchild.harvard.edu/key-concept/brain-architecture/.

35   **He was less hesitant:** "Science of the Brain as a Gateway to Understanding Play: An Interview with Jaak Panksepp," *American Journal of Play* (Winter 2010): 245–77.

35   **For a long time:** Sergio M. Pellis and Stephen M. Siviy, "Introduction to the Special Issue," *International Journal of Play*, 9, no. 1 (2020): 1–3.

35   **"When you put them together":** Quoted in Pamela Weintraub, "Discover Interview: Jaak Panksepp Pinned Down Humanity's 7 Primal Emotions," *Discover*, May 30, 2012, https://www.discover magazine.com/mind/discover-interview-jaak-panksepp-pinned-down -humanitys-7-primal-emotions.

35   **"They played with such eagerness":** "Science of the Brain," *American Journal of Play*, 264.

35   **"If you understand":** Weintraub, "Discover Interview."

36   **"Play allows us to stop":** "Science of the Brain," *American Journal of Play*, 269.

36   **"You can think of curiosity":** Kidd is quoted and science of curiosity discussed in Lydia Denworth, "The Rewards of Curiosity," *Scientific American* 331, no. 5 (2024): 64.

37   **Some of the studies:** Satinder Singh et al., "Intrinsically Motivated Reinforcement Learning: An Evolutionary Perspective," *IEEE Transactions on Autonomous Mental Development* 2, no. 2 (2010): 70–82.

40   **"Playing facilitates growth":** D. W. Winnicott, *Playing and Reality* (Tavistock Publications, 1971), 41. For a summary of Winnicott's thinking, see chap. 3, "Playing: A Theoretical Statement."

40 **Psychologist Teresa Amabile:** Studies described in Peter Gray, *Free to Learn: Why Unleashing the Instinct to Play Will Make Our Children Happier, More Self-Reliant, and Better Students for Life* (Basic Books, 2013), 134–35; and Teresa Amabile, "How Your Work Environment Influences Your Creativity," Center for Positive Organizations, University of Michigan, July 6, 2020, https://positiveorgs.bus.umich.edu/news/how-your-work-environment-influences-your-creativity/.

41 **"Creativity is a spark":** Gray, *Free to Learn*, 135.

41 **Duncker's candle problem:** Study described in Alice M. Isen et al., "Positive Affect Facilitates Creative Problem Solving," *Journal of Personality and Social Psychology* 52, no. 6 (1987): 1122; and Gray, *Free to Learn*, 136–37. Solution: Dump out the tacks and use the cardboard box as a shelf, tacked to the board, then sit the candle on top.

41 **Inspired by her own results:** Described by Kyle Emich in "Remembering Alice M. Isen," Association for Psychological Science, *Observer*, July 18, 2013, https://www.psychologicalscience.org/observer/remembering-alice-isen.

42 **"Whatever I say":** Winnicott, *Playing and Reality*, 40.

42 **"In a tantalizing way":** Winnicott, *Playing and Reality*, 65.

42 **His conclusion:** Winnicott, *Playing and Reality*, 53.

42 **He spoke briefly:** Stuart Brown, "Play Is More Than Just Fun," TED Talk, May 2008.

43 **In August 1966:** Brown, *Play*, 94–97.

44 **"Play is a necessary nutrient":** Stuart Brown at Health & PLAY Consortium, US Play Coalition, April 3, 2022.

44 **"Periodically they paused":** Brown, *Play*, 28.

44 **In fact, it's very difficult:** Aamodt and Wang, *Welcome to Your Child's Brain*, 127.

45 **"herbivores run about":** "Science of the Brain," *American Journal of Play*, 265–70.

47   **I had brought a stack of DIY:** Jay Beckwith and Jeremy Joan Hewes, *Build Your Own Playground!* (Houghton Mifflin, 1974) and M. Paul Friedberg, *Do It Yourself Playgrounds* (Architectural Press, 1975).

50   **Sigmund Freud:** Julie Blundon Nash and Charles E. Schaefer, "Play Therapy: Basic Concepts and Practices," in Charles E. Schaefer, ed., *Foundations of Play Therapy* (John Wiley & Sons, 2011), 4.

51   **"Play is as natural":** Athena A. Drewes and Charles E. Schaefer, "The Therapeutic Powers of Play," in Kevin J. O'Connor et al., eds., *Handbook of Play Therapy* (John Wiley & Sons, 2015), chap. 3.

51   **He identified:** Charles E. Schaefer and Athena A. Drewes, eds., *The Therapeutic Powers of Play: 20 Core Agents of Change* (John Wiley & Sons, 2014).

51   **"A person's play":** Terr, *Beyond Love and Work*, 21.

51   **The cure:** Terr, *Beyond Love and Work*, 206.

52   **A study of adults:** Meredith Van Vleet et al., "The Importance of Having Fun: Daily Play Among Adults with Type 1 Diabetes," *Journal of Social and Personal Relationships* 36, no. 11–12 (2019): 3695–710.

52   **And in children hospitalized for cancer:** María José Godino-Iáñez et al., "Play Therapy as an Intervention in Hospitalized Children: A Systematic Review," *Healthcare* 8, no. 3 (2020): 239.

52   **Laughter heals:** Adrián Pérez-Aranda et al., "Laughing Away the Pain: A Narrative Review of Humour, Sense of Humour and Pain," *European Journal of Pain* 23, no. 2 (2019): 220–33.

3: STAYING PLAYFUL

57   **a woman named Pamela Robinson:** Rozalynn S. Frazier, "Jumping for Joy," *New York Times*, August 19, 2023, https://www.nytimes.com/2023/08/19/well/move/40-double-dutch-club-jump-rope.html.

66   **psychology's Big Five:** Annabelle G. Y. Lim, "Big Five Personality Traits: The 5-Factor Model of Personality," Simply Psychology,

March 20, 2025, https://www.simplypsychology.org/big-five
-personality.html.

66   **The psychologist C. Robert Cloninger:** C. R. Cloninger et al., "A Psychobiological Model of Temperament and Character," *Archives of General Psychiatry* 50, no. 12 (1993): 975–90, doi:10.1001/arch psyc.1993.01820240059008.

69   **Beginning around the age:** Jay N. Giedd, "The Amazing Teen Brain," *Scientific American*, May 2016.

72   **Psychologists now speak of this phase:** Jeffrey Jensen Arnett, "Emerging Adulthood: What Is It, and What Is It Good For?," *Child Development Perspectives* 1, no. 2 (2007): 68–73.

73   **Three-quarters of college graduates:** *Talent Disrupted: Underemployment, College Graduates, and the Way Forward* (Burning Glass Institute and Strada Institute for the Future of Work, 2024).

73   **According to a 2017 report:** *The Next Era of Human-Machine Partnerships: Emerging Technologies' Impact on Society & Work in 2030* (Institute for the Future and Dell Technologies, 2017), https://www.delltechnologies.com/content/dam/delltechnologies /assets/perspectives/2030/pdf/SR1940_IFTFforDellTechnologies _Human-Machine_070517_readerhigh-res.pdf.

74   **In her book:** Julie Lythcott-Haims, *Your Turn: How to Be an Adult* (Henry Holt, 2021), 4–5.

76   **Back in the first half:** Peter Gray, *Free to Learn: Why Unleashing the Instinct to Play Will Make Our Children Happier, More Self-Reliant, and Better Students for Life* (Basic Books, 2013), 7.

76   **In my studio, I've got:** Martha Cooper, *Street Play* (From Here to Fame, 2006).

77   **Between 1981 and 1997:** Gray, *Free to Learn*, 11.

77   **Around the world, we adults:** Charlotte Faircloth, "Intensive Parenting and the Expansion of Parenting," in *Parenting Culture Studies* (Palgrave Macmillan, 2023), https://doi.org/10.1007/978-3 -031-44156-1_2.

78   **journalist Lenore Skenazy wrote:** Lenore Skenazy, "I Let My 9-Year-Old Ride the Subway Alone. I Got Labeled the 'World's Worst Mom,'" *Washington Post*, January 16, 2015, https://www .washingtonpost.com/posteverything/wp/2015/01/16/i-let-my-9-year -old-ride-the-subway-alone-i-got-labeled-the-worlds-worst-mom/.

79   **They mean the baboon:** Jeanne Altmann, *Baboon Mothers and Infants* (University of Chicago Press, 2001), xvi.

79   **Socrates believed:** Neel Burton, *The Gang of Three: Socrates, Plato, Aristotle (Ancient Wisdom)* (Acheron Press, 2024), 86, 132, Kindle; and Paul Johnson, *Socrates: A Man for Our Times* (Viking, 2011), 110, 29–30, Kindle.

80   **"The maturity of man":** Friedrich Nietzsche, *Beyond Good and Evil* (Millennium Publications, 2014), chap. 4.

80   **metamorphoses of the spirit:** Friedrich Nietzsche, "The Three Meta-morphoses," *Thus Spake Zarathustra*, January 26, 2021, https:// www.anthologialitt.com/post/the-three-metamorphoses-by-friedrich -nietzsche.

83   **Play helps us manage:** Brian Sutton-Smith, *Play for Life: Play Theory and Play as Emotional Survival* (The Strong, 2017), 224.

87   **D. W. Winnicott wrote:** Jeffrey S. Applegate, "The Holding Environment: An Organizing Metaphor for Social Work Theory and Practice," *Smith College Studies in Social Work* 68, no. 1 (1997): 7–29, doi:10.1080/00377319709517514.

87   **healer Eduardo Duran:** Discussed in Duran's keynote at Seeking Your Truth: Healing with Wolves conference, Canby, Oregon, June 16–17, 2019. Organized by Wolf Pack Consulting and Therapeutic Services, LLC.

88   **The average age:** Marc Saltzman, "More Adults Play Video Games Than Kids—And More Surprising Stats," *USA Today*, June 11, 2022, https://www.usatoday.com/story/tech/gaming/2022/06/11 /gaming-study-finds-adults-play-more-than-kids/7581101001/.

89   **In a 2015 national poll:** Colleen Walsh, "Keeping Adults in the

Game," *Harvard Gazette*, July 16, 2015, https://news.harvard.edu /gazette/story/2015/07/keeping-adults-in-the-game/.

89 **Studies show that young:** Christina Caron, "This Drinking Habit Is More Dangerous than Bingeing," *New York Times*, November 26, 2024, https://www.nytimes.com/2024/11/26/well/high-intensity -binge-drinking-alcohol.html?searchResultPosition=1.

92 **In an intriguing study:** Elke Schubert and Rainer Strick, "Toy-Free Kindergarten: A Project to Prevent Addiction for Children and with Children," (Aktion Jugendschutz, 1996).

93 **"Friendship is a shortcut":** Tim Brown at Serious Play 2008 now on TED Talks, https://www.ted.com/talks/tim_brown_tales_of _creativity_and_play.

4: MAKING PLAY, NOT TOYS

111 **Prehistoric dice:** Joanna Thompson, "Sticks, Stones and Knucklebones: The History of Dice," HowStuffWorks.com, September 1, 2021, https://entertainment.howstuffworks.com/leisure/traditional -games/history-dice.htm.

111 **An especially cool set:** Rossella Lorenzi, "Oldest Known Gaming Tokens Dug Up in Bronze Age Turkish Graves," NBC News, August 14, 2013, https://www.nbcnews.com/sciencemain/oldest-known -gaming-tokens-dug-bronze-age-turkish-graves-6c10920354.

112 **In his own book:** Steven Johnson, *Wonderland: How Play Made the Modern World* (Penguin Group, 2016), 2–3.

112 **"Because play is often":** Johnson, *Wonderland*, 12–13.

113 **"Toys are like":** Brian Sutton-Smith, "Toys for Object and Role Mastery," in Karen Hewitt and Louise Roomet, eds., *Educational Toys in America: 1800 to the Present* (Robert Hull Fleming Museum, 1979), 11.

114 **It's a central ambiguity:** Brian Sutton-Smith, *The Ambiguity of Play* (Harvard University Press, 1997), 7.

114   **He could plainly see:** Quoted in Sutton-Smith's obituary, Margalit Fox, "Brian Sutton-Smith, Scholar of What's Fun, Dies at 90," *New York Times*, March 15, 2015, https://www.nytimes.com/2015/03/15/science/brian-sutton-smith-scholar-of-whats-fun-dies-at-90.html.

114   **Scholars believe:** John Brewer, "Childhood Revisited: The Genesis of the Modern Toy," in Hewitt and Roomet, *Educational Toys*, 3–10.

114   **As historian John Brewer:** Hewitt and Roomet, *Educational Toys*, 8.

116   **"Why study play?":** Fox, "Brian Sutton-Smith.".

116   **As a result, our view of toys:** Hewitt and Roomet, *Educational Toys*, 12.

117   **In the 1960s and '70s:** Rob Goldberg, *Radical Play: Revolutionizing Children's Toys in 1960s and 1970s America* (Duke University Press, 2023), 2.

117   **"Toymakers were forced":** Goldberg, *Radical Play*, 8.

118   **The previous decades:** Goldberg, *Radical Play*, 5.

121   **Playgrounds were created:** For more on the history of playgrounds, see exhibition catalog by Gabriela Burkhalter, ed., *The Playground Project* (Kunsthalle, JRP/Ringier, 2016); also Naomi Heller, "A Brief History of Playground Design, Parts 1 and 2," The Field, American Society of Landscape Architects, ASLA Professional Practice Networks' Blog, March 12, 2020, https://thefield.asla.org/2020/03/12/a-brief-history-of-playground-design-part-1/.

122   **The architectural playscapes:** Burkhalter, *The Playground Project*, 171–72.

122   **The American architect Richard Dattner:** Burkhalter, *The Playground Project*, 79–80.

123   **A forest is a playground:** For more information, see *School's Out, Lessons from a Forest Kindergarten*, a documentary film by Lisa Molomot and Rona Richter (Linden Tree Films, 2013).

123   **Inspired by children:** Burkhalter, *The Playground Project*, 201–2; and Joan Almon, *Adventure: The Value of Risk in Children's Play* (Alliance for Childhood, 2013), chap. 3.

123 **Marjory Allen, Baroness of Hurtwood:** Burkhalter, *The Playground Project*, 51–52; and Almon, *Adventure*, chap. 3.

127 **"It's a relief to know":** "An Underdog Favorite Makes Toy Hall of Fame," *All Things Considered*, National Public Radio, November 19, 2005.

5: EMBRACE POSSIBILITY

133 **"Knowledge, to a constructivist":** Edith K. Ackermann, "Constructing Knowledge and Transforming the World," in M. Tokoro and L. Steels, eds., *A Learning Zone of One's Own: Sharing Representations and Flow in Collaborative Learning Environments* 1 (2004): 15–37.

135 **Being a playworker:** Penny Wilson, *The Playwork Primer* (Alliance for Childhood, 2010).

136 **"good enough" parents:** D. W. Winnicott, "Transitional Objects and Transitional Phenomena—A Study of the First Not-Me Possession," *International Journal of Psychoanalysis* 34 (1953): 89–97.

136 **"To the adult eye":** *The Land: An Adventure Play Documentary*, produced by Erin Davis (New Day Films, 2015).

137 **I felt the same way:** Sarah Lyon, "Through the Turnstile and Down the Aisle," *New York Times*, October 19, 2024, https://www.nytimes.com/2024/10/19/fashion/weddings/subway-weddings.html.

138 **Design thinking brings:** For more, see IDEO's website, https://designthinking.ideo.com.

139 **Sliding in sideways:** John Cleese, "Creativity in Management," talk, Video Arts, 1991, transcript available on James Clear's website, https://jamesclear.com/great-speeches/creativity-in-management-by-john-cleese#:~:text=What%20I%20am%20suggesting%20to,to%20the%20most%20creative%20solution.

148 **teacher Caroline Pratt:** More on Pratt and her wooden blocks at City and Country website, https://www.cityandcountry.org/history.

151   **In one of the most famous TED:** Sir Ken Robinson, "Do Schools Kill Creativity?" TED Talk, February 2006, https://www.ted.com /talks/sir_ken_robinson_do_schools_kill_creativity?subtitle=en.

152   **"Human flourishing":** Sir Ken Robinson, "Bring on the Learning Revolution," TED Talk, February 2010, https://www.ted.com/talks /sir_ken_robinson_bring_on_the_learning_revolution?subtitle=en.

159   **artist and educator Corita Kent:** Kent's 10 rules are listed on the Corita Art Center website, https://www.corita.org/tenrules.

159   **I post them on classroom:** *TEN RULES for Students and Teachers: Corita on Teaching and Celebration,* a film featuring two documentaries by Baylis Glascock (1967; Baylis Glascock Films, 2007).

162   **A book of advice:** Eric Maisel, *The Art of the Book Proposal: From Focused Idea to Finished Proposal* (Jeremy P. Tarcher/Penguin, 2013), 64–65.

6: RELEASE JUDGMENT

171   **Initially, we called:** Nancy Rudolph, *Workyards: Playgrounds Planned for Adventure* (Teachers College Press, 1974).

178   **As psychotherapist Esther Perel says:** Esther Perel's blog, "How to Introduce Role Play Ideas to Your Partner," estherperel.com, https://www.estherperel.com/blog/how-to-introduce-role-play-ideas -to-your-partner#:~:text=The%20door%20is%20now%20open,can%20 also%20test%20through%20action.

179   **Nearly everyone who takes:** Sample norm violation assignment from Scott Plous at Wesleyan University on Social Psychology Network, https://www.socialpsychology.org/teach/normviolation.htm.

180   **In a study of prevalence:** Margaret E. Tankard and Elizabeth Levy Paluck, "Norm Perception as a Vehicle for Social Change," *Social Issues and Policy Review* 10, no. 1 (2016): 181–211.

181   **When people in parks:** Peter Lovatt, *The Dance Cure: The Surprising Science to Being Smarter, Stronger, Happier* (HarperOne, 2021), 55–56, Kindle.

184   **"Kids say, I can":** Quoted in Gabrielle S. Balkan, "Q+A with To-vah Klein," *Barnard Magazine*, Fall 2019, https://barnard.edu/magazine/fall-2019/qa-tovah-klein#:~:text=Why%20is%20play%20so%20important,the%20foundation%20of%20all%20learning.

184   **As RuPaul says:** RuPaul discusses the phrase with Oprah Win-frey, "RuPaul Explains What 'We're All Born Naked and the Rest Is Drag' Means," SuperSoul Sunday, OWN, January 16, 2018, https://www.youtube.com/watch?v=9RPDSdRCDYs.

187   **When babies babble:** Lenore Terr, *Beyond Love and Work: Why Adults Need to Play* (Simon & Schuster, 1999), 33.

189   **I recently read an article:** Jancee Dunn, "8 Things You Should Never Say to Your Partner, According to Therapists," Well Newsletter, *New York Times*, December 1, 2023, https://www.nytimes.com/2023/12/01/well/family/relationships-counseling-partner-advice.html.

189   **International Training Centre:** You can learn more about the ITC's work at https://www.itcilo.org.

191   **lesson from narrative therapy:** Narrative therapy is described at https://www.psychologytoday.com/us/therapy-types/narrative-therapy.

191   **Stories help human beings:** Jeffrey Kluger, "How Telling Stories Makes Us Human," *Time*, December 5, 2017; and Daniel Smith et al., "Cooperation and the Evolution of Hunter-Gatherer Storytelling," *Nature Communications* 8, no. 1 (2017): 1853.

194   **An example of a corporate:** *Waigaya* is explained in Jeffrey Roth-feder, *Driving Honda: Inside the World's Most Innovative Car Company* (Portfolio, 2014). Adapted by *Strategy + Business*, Autumn 2014, https://www.strategy-business.com/article/00269.

7: REFRAME SUCCESS

197   **"A fiercely non-competitive":** See Pony Sweat Aerobics at https://www.ponysweataerobics.com. For more on Emilia Richeson, see Laura Studarus, "All About Pony Sweat, the Workout That

Teaches You Not to Give a Damn," *Nylon*, June 12, 2017, https:// www.nylon.com/articles/all-about-pony-sweat-emilia-richeson.

200   *Entrepreneurship for Dummies*: Kathleen Allen, *Entrepreneurship for Dummies* (For Dummies, 2000); and Richard C. Levy and Ronald O. Weingartner, *The Toy and Game Inventor's Handbook: Everything You Need to Know to Pitch, License, and Cash-in on Your Ideas* (Alpha, 2003).

201   I saw a story: "Failure Now an Option," *The Onion*, January 16, 2008, https://theonion.com/failure-now-an-option-1819569579/.

202   "I have not failed": See "Famous Quotes by Thomas Edison," Edison Innovation Foundation, https://www.thomasedison.org /edison-quotes.

202   Agatha Christie's first novel: "6 Famous Authors Who Once Faced Rejection," WildMind for Authors, February 22, 2018, https://wildmindcreative.com/bookmarketing/6-famous-authors -who-once-faced-rejection.

202   James Dyson: Madison Malone Kircher, "James Dyson on 5,126 Vacuums That Didn't Work—and the One That Finally Did," *New York*, November 22, 2016, https://nymag.com/vindicated /2016/11/james-dyson-on-5-126-vacuums-that-didnt-work-and-1-that -did.html.

207   Collectively they embrace: For more on Anji Play, visit their website, http://www.anjiplay.com.

209   read the United Nations 1989 Convention: United Nations, Human Rights, Office of the High Commissioner, Convention on the Rights of the Child, adopted November 20, 1989, Article 31.

210   "If the children": Quoted on Anji Play website, http://www.anji play.com.

213   As the Zen master: Shunryū Suzuki, *Zen Mind, Beginner's Mind: Informal Talks on Zen Meditation and Practice* (Weatherhill, 1970).

216   A team of psychologists: Angela Ka-yee Leung et al., "Embodied

Metaphors and Creative 'Acts,'" *Psychological Science* 23, no. 5 (2012): 502–9.

217 **Arakawa and Gins:** For more on Arakawa and Gins' work, see the website of their Reversible Destiny Foundation, https://www .reversibledestiny.org/#.

217 **Peter Lovatt, the psychologist:** Peter Lovatt, *The Dance Cure: The Surprising Science to Being Smarter, Stronger, Happier* (HarperOne, 2021), 107, Kindle.

224 **There is a concept:** For an example of the borderless classroom, see this website created by a Shanghai school: https://theborder lessclassroom.com.

8: BE YOUR OWN PLAYWORKER

234 **"This is the real secret":** Alan Watts speaking on "This is the real secret of life," February 1972, Play.AlanWatts.org, available on YouTube, https://www.youtube.com/shorts/ZuqlWN4imBM.

235 **The playwright S. N. Behrman:** Quoted in Lenore Terr, *Beyond Love and Work: Why Adults Need to Play* (Simon & Schuster, 1999), 30.

237 **Like Emma Goldman:** Goldman is widely credited with saying she didn't want to be part of a revolution that didn't allow dancing. That's not quite accurate, but she did say something like it. Alix Kates Shulman, "Invention of a Feminist Sound Bite," *Lilith*, December 24, 2001, http://lilith.org/articles/invention-of-a-feminist -sound-bite//.

243 **"Play is a lost key":** Terr, *Beyond Love and Work*, 40.

248 *Richard Scarry's Busy, Busy Town:* Richard Scarry, *Richard Scarry's Busy, Busy Town* (Golden Books, 2000).

INDEX